TEACHING THE MATURE RIDER

Moulton
College

NORTHAMPTONSHIRE

Profit through Skill

Teaching the Mature Rider

Martin Diggle

with cartoons by
Anne Pilgrim

J. A. ALLEN & CO.
LONDON

British Library Cataloguing-in-Publication Data
A catalogue record for this book is available from the British Library.

ISBN 0-85131-553-4

Published in Great Britain in 1993 by
J. A. Allen & Company Limited
1 Lower Grosvenor Place
London SW1W 0EL

Printed in Great Britain by
St Edmundsbury Press Limited, Bury St Edmunds, Suffolk.

Contents

List of Illustrations

List of Cartoons

Acknowledgement

The author wishes to acknowledge with thanks the contribution of Marian Pattison, BHSII, who drew on her wealth of experience to identify and highlight many of the ideas addressed in this book.

Foreword

This book has been written in recognition of the fact that an increasing number of people now learn to ride when well into adulthood. Its purpose is to identify the problems – and advantages – that this can produce for both pupils and instructors, and to encourage the latter to give them due consideration. Its primary concern, therefore, is not with the technicalities of riding instruction, but with understanding and communication.

The ideas in this work are based on extensive observation of, and discussion with, adult riders and their teachers, and on considerable personal involvement with a club that has pursued an active policy of encouraging adult beginners.

I hope that these ideas will assist instructors to maximise the effectiveness of their teaching, and consequently benefit those they teach.

Introduction

Defining the Mature Rider

'Mature' is a rather broad term that has been used to define, among other things, a highly desirable state in cheese. In a human context it might be defined as 'fully adult' but, while such a definition could cover post-puberty to old age, maturity is more commonly used to describe the middle ground between 'young adult' and 'elderly'. It is with the latter usage in mind that the term is employed in this book, and I would add a further personal definition of a mature rider being one who has passed his or her athletic peak; that is to say, having reached an age at which the *physical* powers in athletic sports have begun to decline. Since a number of factors are involved here, it would be unrealistic to suggest a precise age at which riders reach 'maturity'. However, it may be of interest – if not scientific significance – to note that many veteran rider classes at shows have a lower age limit of 35, and it is with riders of the 'late thirties' onward that this book is chiefly concerned.

I should also add that it is more specifically concerned with teaching mature beginners and novices than those people who have ridden consistently since youth. Although their experience will not necessarily immunise the latter from the problems of their non-riding peers, they will have already absorbed the basics (which tends to get physically harder with age), and they should have been able to adapt gradually to various physical conditions that would be more disruptive if already established in someone starting from scratch. There is, however, an exception to this point: while, *as a group*, experienced mature riders may have these advantages, there may be *individuals* who encounter considerable difficulties in, for example, coming to terms with the effects of a sudden injury or affliction that interferes with a riding style that has developed over a number of years. Such individuals will require extra assistance and encouragement from their teacher, and, providing it can be regarded as a considerable and worthwhile challenge.

Why Mature Riders Need Special Consideration
If we accept that the basic principles of riding apply to all, and that many of the attributes of 'maturity' in pupils might be considered generally helpful by their teachers, we might then ask why it should be necessary to give special consideration to teaching the mature rider. The fundamental answer to this question is rooted in the fact that effective riding requires a sound intellectual understanding of the principles of good riding, matched with the physical ability to put them into practice. Where these assets are not fully developed, or are impaired or unbalanced, the teaching and learning processes will inevitably be more difficult. These realities are pretty ‚obvious in some areas (for example, teaching disabled riders and younger children) but where they are acknowledged by competent teachers, the results can be remarkable.

Where 'mature' riders are involved, however, there can often be a more subtle imbalance, with pupils being at the height of their intellectual powers, but past their physical peak. In saying this, I am not seeking to portray all riders over 40 as infirm sages, I am simply suggesting that a general tendency for instructors to treat all adults as though they are young and fit is unrealistic. Furthermore, the possibility exists that teachers who can overlook potential weaknesses in pupils may also overlook potential strengths, to the double detriment of their instruction. While this is true for pupils of all ages and conditions, let us look in more detail at the ramifications for instructing the mature rider.

CHAPTER ONE

The Mature Pupil: Background Influences

Discovering Motivation

In any teaching process it is highly advantageous for the instructor to understand the pupils' motivations and ambitions, as this information will indicate, in broad terms, what they expect to be taught and how receptive they are likely to be. The way to find out about pupils' motivations and ambitions, of course, is by talking to them, but varying circumstances may require different approaches. It is easiest to do this when giving individual tuition, as there is often less pressure of time, and the pupil may readily volunteer such information, perhaps even having booked the lesson with a particular goal or ambition in mind. In such circumstances, the instructor may legitimately spend part of the lesson discussing the pupil's riding in the light of a declared ambition; for example, explaining the importance of attention to flatwork to a pupil with showjumping aspirations.

It is obviously harder to go into detailed discussion with one pupil in a group lesson, when others are keen to get on with riding. However, instructors should try never to ignore completely any relevant question or observation from a pupil during a lesson, and he or she should also try, at all times, to involve all pupils, so that individuals learn

1

from the whole lesson, rather than only from what is directed specifically at them. Where such an approach is accepted by the pupils, the chances of regular dialogue are greatly increased, and there is more likelihood of pupils 'opening up' about their backgrounds and aims. In addition to providing the teacher with relevant information, this state of affairs is generally more encouraging than giving a lesson where there is no feedback, and having the end of lesson 'any questions?' met by stony silence. The only points to beware of when adopting this approach are that the conversation is not hogged by one particularly talkative pupil, and that talking does not become a *substitute* for riding. Such situations are, however, readily circumvented; in the first instance by tact, and in the second by the instructor retaining a balance between theory and practice.

There may, of course, be moments outside lessons when the opportunity arises to chat to pupils. Although an instructor should not adopt a policy of constant interrogation, an occasional casually worded question may elicit useful information about a pupil's motives and aspirations. For example, a question along the lines of 'How did you get involved in this strange sport?' may produce an answer that makes reference to other sporting activities, family involvement and so on. A question such as 'Are you hoping to do a bit of competing in due course?' may trigger statements of ambition, or perhaps allow the instructor to fan the flames of this by explaining that many forms of competitive riding are within the compass of the 'ordinary' rider.

Reasons Why Mature People Take Up Riding
The main reasons are:
1) It is something they have wanted to do for a long while,

but they have previously lacked the time/money/opportunity.
2) They have become interested through the influence of family or friends.
3) Some form of impulse, or through a general desire to 'try something different'.
4) Desire/medical advice to take gentle exercise.
5) Short-term expediency (for example, an actor preparing for a role in which he or she has to appear on horseback, or someone who has booked a riding holiday on a whim, and wants to 'get in some practise').

One consequence of an instructor's desire to understand motivation is a tendency to make preliminary estimates of a pupil's likely keenness on the basis of the reasons he or she has given for taking up the sport. In many cases there are strong links between these factors but, before discussing them, it should be stressed that such estimates should not be used as a basis for dismissive prejudgement. Some of the reasons given may sound distinctly unpromising, and it is quite realistic to acknowledge that a proportion of pupils will, for various reasons beyond the instructor's control, be limited in their enthusiasm and commitment. These facts do not, however, excuse consequential lack of such qualities on the part of the instructor. Such attitudes are not simply unprofessional; they can materially increase the risk of an accident, and will *confirm* loss of enthusiasm in pupils, whereas the instructor's role should be to inspire – or at least to attempt to. As long as an instructor remains prepared to teach a pupil, he or she should do so with full commitment, however much of an uphill struggle this may sometimes seem.

This said, it remains useful to consider, in broad terms,

how pupils' initial motivations are likely to influence their enthusiasm. Generally speaking, those who start riding for the first reason are likely to be the most keen and if they have harboured a deep and long-frustrated desire, they may well exhibit a degree of enthusiasm that would shame many career students. Such enthusiasm may or may not be supported by other assets but as it is, of itself, the asset that is most fundamentally important in any learning process, every attempt should be made to foster and encourage it.

The influence of family and friends should not be underestimated. Although, in some cases, it may simply induce a light-hearted decision to 'have a go', it may also act as a trigger for a subconscious desire – indeed, if *some* desire did not already exist, it is unlikely that such influences would have any effect. It is surprising how many people start riding in their middle years as a result of sustained 'ear bashing' from teenage progeny, and then go on to develop a depth of interest that outlasts that of their offspring.

Of those who start riding through impulse, or a desire to 'try something different', there may be a proportion who become genuinely interested but, in many cases, the probability is that enthusiasm will wane. This is especially likely in cases where people have a history of flitting from sport to sport, as opposed to being genuinely interested in several sports. Such people often look upon sports simply as casual pastimes, or are seeking an area in which they can achieve instant success. They frequently lack the commitment necessary to become proficient at any sport, which is one reason why they are so ready to move on to another. It is usually people from this group whose unrealistic ambitions can cause difficulties for their instructors, an issue we shall examine shortly.

Those who take up riding with the chief intention of

gaining gentle exercise can be considered, by definition, as recreational riders. These people may suffer from some physical condition that would make it difficult for them to participate in the more rigorous equestrian sports, but this does not necessarily preclude them from being interested in, and enthusiastic about, what they do; indeed some of these riders may be frustrated by the restrictions under which they have to operate. That such people require – and are worthy of – careful consideration will be apparent to anyone who has had dealings with riders who are actually handicapped.

People who seek riding instruction as a short-term expedient are something of a special case and, by definition, it will prove exceptional if they decide to continue the sport on a permanent basis. This does not mean, however, that they will necessarily lack enthusiasm. Indeed, the actor cited earlier may be very keen because the success of his or her role may depend on the ability to ride well.

If such clients are taken on, it must be on the basis that the instructor acknowledges their special requirements and is prepared to work in context; a pupil who needs to learn enough to canter safely across a couple of fields will not need or welcome a lesson spent on riding turns on the forehand. This said, the instructor must still insist that the pupil makes available sufficient time to gain a preliminary understanding of the basic principles of riding, and achieves a degree of security independent of the reins. Without these assets, the instructor has no basis from which to teach the pupil's specific requirements, while the pupil, once beyond the confines of the teaching arena, will be helpless. Because of the nature of this type of instruction, it is usually best to do the preliminary work on the lunge, and, with the emphasis on special needs, all tuition should be on a one-to-one basis.

The case of a potential holidaymaker is somewhat different; rather than having a professional requirement to learn a new skill, he or she is acting on a short-term whim. Being aware of what learning to ride entails, the instructor may be amazed that anyone should consider such casual involvement. However, it must be borne in mind that the client is in the converse position; because he or she does not ride, he or she does not realise what is involved. He or she may, in fact, perceive the venture in the same light as someone booking a first skiing holiday and having a couple of dry-slope lessons before departing. He or she may also consider that, far from indicating ignorance, the fact that he or she is seeking a little instruction is evidence of enlightenment and, indeed, there is some truth in this.

When confronted by such a potential pupil, the instructor should first ascertain the type of holiday envisaged and, in the light of this information, advise on the practicalities. Should the instructor believe the venture to be dangerously unsuitable, he or she should try to dissuade the client from proceeding, and should not become embroiled in (perhaps literally) a 'crash course' by attempting to teach too much in an impossibly short time. If, on the other hand, the proposals are not too unrealistic, there is no reason why the pupil should not follow the same type of programme as any other beginner. In view of their requirements, any extra sessions such pupils can spend on the lunge will obviously be beneficial while, if circumstances permit, some experience of riding in the open (in safe surroundings, under escort) will help their cause. They may also have reason to be grateful for a rudimentary grounding in such matters as basic handling of horses, grooming and tacking up.

Ambitions

However strong their enthusiasm, the majority of mature riders can be expected to express less flamboyant ambition than may be the case with their younger counterparts. Typical attitudes will be along the lines of 'I'd just like to become good enough to enjoy myself', or 'I fancy having a go at jumping in due course, but let's see how I get on with the basics first'. In some instances, there may be an element of understatement from people who do not wish to look foolish but, in the main, such expressions of ambition are reasonably realistic. Such realism is, essentially, a mark of mature thinking, and can actually be more helpful to both pupil and teacher than the wild hopes of youngsters, who so readily declare their intentions to follow in the footsteps of the last person to win Badminton. This is not to say that there is anything intrinsically wrong with great ambition, it is simply that, unstructured and unsupported, it lays the foundation for frequent disappointment, whereas a pro-gramme of modest progression affords a high probability of modest successes, each of which bolsters confidence and enthusiasm.

In general, then, an instructor should welcome the modest ambitions expressed by the majority of mature pupils, bearing in mind that, as they are not impatient to excel, they may well pay more heed to achieving a sound understanding of the basics than is often the case with impetuous youngsters. What the instructor *must not* do, however, is misinterpret modest declarations of ambition and provide half-hearted, condescending tuition on the grounds that the pupils 'are never going to be any good anyway'. Apart from the other ramifications, this is an insult to such clients' intelligence. In many cases, although novices in the field of riding, they may be well versed in buying goods and services and will not take kindly to being 'shortchanged'. Should they suspect that such is the case, the instructor may swiftly and deservedly lose his or her clientele.

Of course, not all mature riders begin with modest aims and ambitions. I have already mentioned those who have long harboured a desire to ride and this group, especially, will sometimes include a pupil with serious ambitions. Although such people will be in a hurry in the sense that they have had to wait for this moment and realise that they have limited time in which to achieve their goals, they are unlikely to exhibit the dismissive impatience associated with youth. In most cases, they will have the mental maturity to recognise that they cannot afford to waste time in misunderstanding the basics and running up blind alleys, and they will, therefore, be hardworking, self-critical and attentive. Such pupils deserve, and should get, every possible assistance from the instructor, both for altruistic reasons and because their successes will do the teacher's reputation nothing but good.

The other side of this coin is, however, represented by those (fortunately rare) people who *do* assume they can obtain instant success and *do not* possess such sensible attributes. These people tend to divide into two groups: those who respond to various examples of human en-deavour by claiming, 'I could do that', without having any perception of the skills involved, and those who believe that throwing enough money at any project will guarantee success.

Of the first group, the majority will exhibit an initial enthusiasm and then vanish in a cloud of excuses when confronted by reality. Just occasionally, however, such a person may become genuinely captivated, admit ruefully that 'It's not as easy as it looks', and start to apply themselves with the zeal of the converted. From an instructor's point of view, this group, while mildly exasperating, is largely self-regulating; to put it bluntly, they will either give up or shape up.

It is in the second group that instructors are more likely to find pupils who are a real trial. There is a world of difference between those who decide to pursue a specific equestrian interest, realise the need to learn to ride first and apply themselves and their finances assiduously to that end, and those who feel that their financial status entitles them to omit the initial learning process altogether. The latter, typically, will spend several thousand pounds on a horse, then expect assistance with their chosen discipline within an unrealistic timescale and on an unrealistic basis ('I don't want riding lessons – I just want to do dressage').

Naturally, an instructor should put his or her best efforts towards persuading such clients of the benefits of a more realistic approach; but, if clients fail to adopt this or become involved at too late a stage, the prognosis is not good. The probable scenario is a period of frustration in which the pupils will blame the horse, its vendor and the instructor, but never themselves, while the instructor finds his or her natural sympathies increasingly directing all energies toward limiting damage to the horse. In such circumstances the freelance instructor will have to make the decision as to whether he or she needs the fee that badly. An employed instructor will have the harder task of maintaining a professional attitude towards such clients, while keeping private the earnest wish that they take their custom elsewhere. In this respect, while I would reiterate that an instructor is never justified in offering poor 'value', the fact remains that teaching has to be received as well as given, and the

'I don't want lessons. I just want to do dressage'

instructor of adults can only offer services; the client cannot be coerced into accepting them.

Sporting Influences
Those who begin riding in maturity may have all sorts of sporting backgrounds, or none at all. Although no other sport provides particularly good specific preparation for riding, any activity can be considered beneficial if it

promotes one or more of the following: general fitness (especially strong legs and a supple spine), sense of balance, general co-ordination, understanding of the importance of correct posture. It should also be said that experience of sports which involve falling over as a routine part of the activity may be useful in minimising damage in the event of a riding accident.

In general terms, experience of being coached in any physical activity is helpful, as, to a lesser extent, is recent experience of receiving tuition of any kind. (It is possible to get out of the habit of being taught.) In the early stages of riding, competitive instinct, in the form of a desire to beat others, is of little value, but a desire for personal improvement (competing against one's own standards) certainly is; again, this is not necessarily confined to physical sports.

Not all sporting influences are wholly beneficial. Some, such as old sporting injuries which impair the capacity to ride well, are patently counterproductive, but there are also those that have the potential to act as two-edged swords. For example, a pupil who has a background of cycle or motorbike racing would benefit in terms of fitness and balance, but *might* have an inherent tendency to try to ride a horse as though it were a bike. Although instructors should not develop neuroses about such possibilities, it is worth bearing them in mind as an aid to prevention – or at least early diagnosis – of pupil errors.

It is also worth remembering that if teacher and pupil share a common interest in some other sport, the former may be able to draw useful analogies to illustrate instructional points.

In cases where pupils have no significant sporting background, an instructor should be wary of making prejudgements solely on this basis. It is, for instance, perfectly feasible for someone to keep fit through an active occupation, and lack of sporting endeavour does not *necessarily* indicate lack of balance, co-ordination and so on. Furthermore, because riding is so different, success at other sports does not necessarily indicate that a pupil will have a natural aptitude for riding, nor does a lack of interest or success in other sports indicate that he or she will not. It might, in fact, be argued that if riding is the first sport in which a pupil has taken a real, voluntary interest, then that interest could prove to be exceptionally intense.

Pupils Returning to Riding After a Long Layoff

On occasion, an instructor may meet a pupil who is returning to riding after a layoff of many years. In such cases, it will be helpful to ascertain how much the pupil did in the past, why he or she gave up and what has motivated him or her to start again. Generally speaking, someone who rode a little in childhood and then moved on to other interests is more likely to be coming back 'for fun', perhaps through family influences, whereas someone who was very keen but was forced to give up through changes in circumstances may well find the old fires rekindling – however lowkey their initial ambitions on returning to the saddle. While, in general, past experience can be considered helpful to both pupil and teacher, there are certain important points to bear in mind:

1) If a pupil's previous experience was very limited and they were either untaught or badly taught, they will probably be worse off than a complete beginner, and may have to 'unlearn' various misconceptions and errors. However, it is important to remember that pupils may draw confidence from what they believe is a small store of knowledge, and this must not be brutally demolished;

the instructor's task is to re-educate, not to make pupils feel foolish.

2) Especially if a pupil's previous experience was a long time ago, there may be complications over changes in style. Like all sports, riding is subject to both superficial fads and more serious changes in technical thinking, and it is quite possible that a pupil may claim that something he or she is being told is at odds with previous teaching. In such cases, clear, rational explanation of the new philosophy is called for in order to avoid confusion and resentment of the 'I spent years being told to do this, and now I'm told it's all wrong' type. Also, of course, the instructor must be certain that it is his or her method, and not the old one, that is appropriate – 'change' and 'progress' are not necessarily synonymous!

Mention of what is appropriate brings us to a consideration of differences in style that relate not so much to time but to circumstance. If, for example, a pupil with past experience in racing wishes to learn dressage and showjumping, it will be necessary to make significant changes to his or her posture and style. This is not a matter of the previous style being wrong, simply that it was specialised and would be unsuited to the new disciplines. It is important that the instructor makes it clear to the pupil that he or she appreciates such distinctions, and is not being dismissive of the pupil's specialised skills. Similarly, a pupil whose former experience consisted entirely of hunting over difficult terrain, might have a style lacking refinement in various areas. However, while it would be incumbent upon the teacher to provide this refinement, he or she should not ignore useful attributes such as fearlessness and the general ability to exercise control. The instructor's role, indeed, would be to *add* polish to such qualities, and certainly not to propose any measures likely to compromise them.

3) It must be of particular concern to a teacher if a pupil who rode in the past gave up through loss of confidence. This can happen for a variety of reasons, but is usually rooted in a frightening experience (or series thereof) with which the rider was unable to cope, perhaps coupled with a serious injury. Helpfully for the instructor, a pupil who admits to loss of confidence is usually willing to divulge the reasons and genuinely keen for the lost confidence to be restored – indeed, this is indicated by the very fact that he or she is prepared to make a fresh attempt. Since the problem is not necessarily confined to novice riders, the instructor should listen carefully to any explanations given, but should refrain from presuming any links between confidence and competence until there has been an opportunity to assess the technical ability of the pupil (making due distinction between 'rustiness', nervousness or lack of knowledge or skill).

Generally speaking, restoring confidence is more straightforward in novice riders than the more experienced. The main reason for this is that the very inexperience of the former increases the chances of them being unable to cope with a difficulty should it arise. This, of course, is no reflection on the riders; it may simply be that the problem arose too early in their riding career – they may even be the victims of an error of judgement on the part of a former teacher, escort or hirer. In such cases, given that the riders did not possess the knowledge or ability to deal with the problem, they could not reasonably be expected to have the *confidence* to do so, and thus have no grounds for the self-recrimination that often goes hand-in-glove with loss of confidence. If such pupils can be persuaded of this, and the instructor can impart the required skills in a logical and measured fashion, there is no reason why confidence should not be restored and consolidated.

However, when experienced riders lose confidence, the basic premise is often reversed, in that their experience *increases* the probability – or at least the assumption – that they *will* be able to cope with most difficulties. Thus, if a situation arises where they cannot, the blow to their confidence may be greater than in the case of inexperienced riders. Because of their overall experience, loss of confidence is likely to be partial rather than total but if it interferes with participation in a chosen discipline, a combination of disappointment, disillusionment and sometimes self-disgust can lead to a decision to give up altogether.

In such circumstances, it may be much harder for the instructor to give specific advice on the root cause of the loss of confidence, so the first aim should be to get the pupil enjoying riding once more. One common symptom of loss of confidence is that the victim becomes overly self-critical and will not acknowledge his or her own strengths. The instructor can assist here by doing this on the pupil's behalf, but he or she must be sure that what is being praised is genuinely praiseworthy, since such pupils will react adversely to anything that hints of condescension. The instructor can avoid such a reaction and win the pupil's confidence and respect, by making sure that he or she picks up any minor errors, and takes an 'it's good, but we can improve it' attitude. Such an approach should gradually help to improve the pupil's self-image. He or she should begin to realise that whatever traumas have occurred he or she is actually quite an able rider. In due course, the pupil may make his or her own decision to confront the cause of the problem, at which juncture the instructor must refrain at all cost from saying 'About time' and dropping the pupil in at the deep end. Instead, he or she should be quietly encouraging, if anything lagging slightly behind the pupil in apparent enthusiasm, and the instructor must also, of course, give the best technical advice of which he or she is capable.

CHAPTER TWO

Establishing Good
Pupil/Teacher Relationships

The fundamental factor in establishing a good pupil/ teacher relationship is the mutual acknowledgement that both have a common goal, which is that the pupil becomes proficient.

Among young pupils there is often no conscious recognition of this philosophy; their perceptions of the educational process may be coloured by having various subjects thrust upon them willy-nilly at school. While they are certainly enthusiastic about subjects they 'enjoy', their likes and dislikes of subjects and teachers tend to have strong correlations, and are also closely linked to their natural aptitude. Given an option, therefore, the fundamental requirement of young pupils is enjoyment. If they enjoy themselves, the desire for improvement will be stimulated, and their attention paid to, and respect for, the teacher will increase.

Although such attitudes will not entirely disappear with age, a mature person will usually have a more pragmatic approach to the teaching/learning process. Many mature pupils will have had experience of teaching or of training staff, and will be fully aware that the end purpose of training is to produce someone competent to function efficiently without constant supervision. Many, again, will be parents who are engaged in encouraging their children towards intelligent, independent-minded adulthood, and who will draw upon their own experiences in matters of formal education.

Therefore, while mature pupils will recognise the value of enjoyment in learning, and would prefer it to be part of their own experiences, their basic requirement is that they *learn*, and they will seek tacit assurances from their teacher's attitude that this is likely to happen. It is a mistake for a teacher of mature riders to appear too slapdash or uncommitted, and it is also a (regrettably common) error to appear condescending. Rather, the perception pupils should have of their instructor is of someone whose attitude says, 'I respect your desire to learn to ride, I can help you to become competent and we can do this in a friendly and informal way'. In addition to reassuring the keener and more ambitious pupils, this attitude should also encourage those who are more diffident to re-evaluate their aims.

Communication
If communication between teacher and pupils is to be fully effective, there must be as few barriers to this as possible. Barriers to effective communication may arise through differences between people; of age, background, character, attitudes and so on. While there can be numerous permutations of such factors, it may be helpful to examine some common possibilities, on the grounds that awareness can help to avoid or minimise them.

AGE
Age is a prime example of a factor that need not create problems, but has an enormous capacity for doing so. The main reason for this is that an age gap can be at the root of

'Thank you Lucinda – we're discussing the forward seat *next* week'

many differences in experience, social status, attitudes, forms of expression and so on.

There is a considerable element of truth in the idea that age lends authority: in mature circles, this is largely due to a respect for the experience it should bring. Where teaching mature riders is concerned, the potential difficulty is that, not infrequently, the pupils may be old enough to be their instructor's parents, and there is a consequent possibility of awkwardness and embarrassment on both sides. Attempts to cover this up may manifest themselves in mutual silliness. On the one hand, it is possible that pupils who are 'ageing' rather than 'mature', and who are 'playing at' riding, may adopt a patronising attitude towards their instructor. This, essentially, is a comment on their own inadequacies, and the instructor must not react by indulging in sarcasm or, worse, engineering or allowing a situation to arise that will 'take so-and-so down a peg or two'. Such behaviour is unprofessional, potentially dangerous and belongs in the school playground rather than the teaching arena. Instead, the teacher should maintain an air of calm maturity, and allow any such pupils to embarrass themselves into silence or compliance, which, sooner or later, they will do.

The other side of the silliness coin is the teacher who tries to compensate for youthfulness by adopting an 'I know more than you' attitude toward the pupils. This will merely reinforce any suspicion about the teacher's immaturity in the minds of the pupils, whose response – spoken or otherwise – will be 'We know that – that's why we're paying you to teach us – so get on with it.'

For the younger teacher, the best approach is to realise that sensible mature people will accept the disparity in age as long as the teacher behaves in an adult fashion and is proficient. A corollary to this – and the antithesis of teacher condescension – is that an instructor should not be in awe of his or her pupil on the grounds of age, wealth, fame or status. It should be remembered that the horse is a great leveller, a pupil is a pupil, and it is an instructor's business to instruct.

Another example of age creating a barrier may arise in a class of mixed ages, where there is only one mature pupil. (For various reasons, this is not ideal, but it may be something over which the instructor has no control.) In such circumstances, any barrier is not directly between pupil and teacher, but between pupil and the environment; the older pupil may feel awkward and out of place, especially if most of the other pupils are more advanced. An instructor can help to overcome this with diplomacy; he or she must treat all pupils as though they were fully mature, should avoid group movements of a kind that might cause the mature pupil to try too hard to keep up, and should avoid any mounted exercises of a type that might make the mature rider feel foolish.

BACKGROUND

There is no room for snobbery in riding, on the part of either teacher or pupil. However, people do, inevitably, come from and move in different circles, and they readily come to look upon certain mannerisms, accents, phrases and idioms as their personal 'norms'. Any marked variations from such 'norms' will tend to create initial barriers to communication, and a sensitive communicator will recognise this and adapt accordingly. The essence of such adaptation is subtlety, without which the effect may be gauche or even offensive. An instructor's aim in such cases should be, essentially, to avoid any extreme mannerisms on his or her own part, and not to attempt a third-rate mimicry of the pupils. Furthermore, an instructor can avoid attracting any snobbish reaction from pupils by ensuring that he or she is, at all times, articulate, audible and at least moderately presentable. In addition to the first two factors being essential for controlling and instructing a ride, it should be realised that slovenliness, in any form, will tend to undermine a teacher's authority.

CHARACTER AND TEMPERAMENT

Natural differences in character and temperament can create

perhaps the hardest barriers to overcome, as it is difficult for anyone – pupil or teacher – to sublimate such fundamental traits. However, while communication is a two-way issue, it is the teacher who must take the ultimate responsibility for establishing and maintaining it, and who must therefore ensure that he or she does not provoke or encourage any 'personality clashes'. This is not to say that the teacher should defer in all things to the pupils; what we are concerned with is avoiding loss of empathy, perhaps by adopting too brisk an attitude with an easygoing pupil, or being lackadaisical with an impatient, intense one.

It is, of course, possible that an instructor may very occasionally form an actual dislike of certain pupils. In all but the most exceptional circumstances, however, it is the instructor's duty to conceal this fact. Exceptional circumstances would include:

> Pupils persistently endangering themselves or other riders or horses through ignoring or disobeying instructions.
>
> Wilful or persistent abuse of the horse.

In the event of such occurrences, an instructor is obliged to take firm action, but it is inappropriate to resort to personal abuse. If the situation permits, the instructor should speak to such pupils privately after the lesson, state fully and clearly the cause for concern, and suggest that if they are unable or unwilling to follow instructions then their future attendance is pointless. Such action should result in either a (let us hope sincere) apology, which will close the matter, or the immediate and unmourned loss of the clients concerned. Where instructors doubt that their terms of employment empower them to take such steps in person, they should refer the matter promptly to the stable proprietor, who should take the same action. (A proprietor who is not prepared to back his

or her staff and/or *needs* an obnoxious client, is a poor bet as
an employer.)

Should a pupil's behaviour be so unacceptable that he or
she cannot be allowed to complete a lesson, the ride should
be halted, the pupil asked to dismount, and the instructor
should lead the horse from the arena, requesting that the
pupil follow. The pupil should then be told the reasons for
this action, offered (if appropriate) a refund of his or her fee,
and told that any future patronage is unwanted. Such action
can be embarrassing and unpleasant, but the need for it is
extremely rare. In riding instruction, as with any other
business, there are always, regrettably, a few clients without whom one is better off.

The Value of Humour
Leaving aside these unpleasant considerations, let us look at
a lighter aspect of communication. Getting people to laugh
with you is a great help in breaking down communication
barriers; it relaxes all parties and indicates that, however
serious one may be about one's subject, one does not take
oneself too seriously. A sense of humour can, therefore, be
a considerable asset in a riding instructor – indeed, it has
wisely been identified as essential in anyone who has any
dealings with horses. However, humour is always best
when natural. There are few things less funny than somebody desperately trying to make others laugh, and a painful
attempt to turn oneself into a stand-up comic who teaches
riding is doomed to embarrassing failure. ('The only funny
thing about . . . is that he thinks he's a riding instructor.')

For a naturally humorous person, however, this gift can
be useful, but it is still necessary to adhere to certain
guidelines. The first and fundamental one is to remember
that one's main function is to teach people, not to take the

mickey out of them, and that what might pass for witty repartee among close friends may give offence to a paying client. An instructor should, therefore, avoid 'hard-edged' humour, sarcasm, 'gallows humour' ('You'll be riding so-and-so, so I'll take your money now') and personal remarks, and he or she should *never* make fun of a pupil who has fallen off or lost control.

Humour is of the greatest value in tuition when it serves to illustrate or underline a serious point. How this is done will vary according to individuals and circumstances, but I can cite a particularly good example from my own experience. A friend of mine – an excellent teacher in all respects – enhances his instruction with his repertoire of horse impressions. These are not given in isolation, but as an integral part of his explanation of the consequences of incorrect riding. However, in addition to reproducing incorrect movement, he also imitates – with remarkable accuracy – the facial expressions of disgruntled equines. These impressions cause much amusement, but also provide a powerful and lasting image, and it is certain that no right-thinking pupil would want his or her horse to look like my friend does when there is too much 'contact' on his 'inside rein'.

CHAPTER THREE

Physical Considerations

While an instructor should take account of the physical condition of *any* pupil, extra consideration is necessary when teaching mature people, especially when they are new pupils. Although there may be those who are in excellent shape, mature people, as a group, have had a fair time to succumb to general 'wear and tear'; ironically, it is quite conceivable that pupils who have kept very fit through rigorous sporting activity, may carry some sport-related injury that impairs their riding. It is also conceivable that someone who has pursued certain sports (for example weightlifting) to a high level, may be muscle-bound to a degree where suppleness is lost.

As far as the unfit are concerned, their lack of fitness may be deep-rooted in a long period of sedentary lifestyle, and they may find even moderate physical effort highly taxing. A further by-product of a sedentary desk job may be the development of a 'round-shouldered' posture which, if uncorrected, will prove very detrimental when riding.

Given such realities, it is important that an instructor acknowledges them and works with the raw material he or she has been given. In doing this, there will be three major considerations.

1) Purely physical or preventive: avoiding aggravating existing damage, or causing new problems through ignoring it.

2) Understanding that a physical problem may prevent a pupil from putting into practice a principle of which he or she has a sound intellectual grasp; being sympathetic to the frustration this may cause the pupil – and avoiding displaying any frustration that it may cause for the teacher!
3) Wherever possible, working around existing problems and/or suggesting ways to alleviate them, if the possibility exists.

While most instructors will not be able to evaluate pupils' infirmities in the manner of a qualified medical practitioner, it is essential that they understand *in riding terms* the general consequences of broad types of impediment, in order that their teaching takes these factors into account. To give a common example, if a pupil has 'back trouble' (especially of the lower back), an instructor will risk aggravating it if he or she insists upon prolonged periods of sitting trot on a horse with a jarring action. He or she will also risk aggravating this condition by expecting the pupil to ride at speed on a horse that 'takes a hold'; it may cause all sorts of new problems if the pupil's back 'gives out' and he or she loses control.

The instructor must also be aware that lower back problems will almost inevitably lessen the effectiveness with which a pupil can use the seat and back – however well he or she may understand the underlying principles. Therefore, the instructor must adapt his or her own demands – and perhaps help to modify the pupil's goals – accordingly and, as far as possible, work around the problem by ensuring that the pupil rides comfortable horses.

Other conditions where common sense can maximise

instructional value while minimising discomfort and risk include:

Hip Problems
The instructor should take care regarding the leg position demanded, and consider the pupil's comfort and security in conjunction with the effectiveness of the aids. He or she should avoid mounting pupils with hip trouble on unduly wide horses – indeed, mounting small, narrow-hipped riders on large, wide horses can *induce* hip problems and thigh strain.

Care must be taken over the amount of trot work demanded (especially rising trot), and the instructor should ensure that the pupil can cope with the associated postural adaptations before galloping and jumping.

Damage to Other Joints/Arthritic Conditions
Damage to joints can reduce flexibility and thus the precision and effectiveness of the aids, and this must be taken into account as indicated by individual cases. Generally speaking, it may help those afflicted if they can ride one of those clever old horses that has learnt to 'interpret' a variety of aids. Arthritis of the hands can affect a rider's ability to hold the reins correctly and securely, with all the difficulty that this implies in giving rein aids.

Damage to/Long-standing Weakness of Muscles/Tendons/Ligaments
As far as possible, avoid stressing affected areas. (Bear in mind that if such tissues actually tear while riding, the pain may well render the rider helpless.) When such problems occur in the leg, it may be difficult and uncomfortable for a pupil to ride with the leathers correctly shortened for

jumping or galloping; this may influence how much is done and perhaps the choice of horse. In some cases, the use of support bandages may help to alleviate the problem.

Predisposition to Cramp
Bad cramp can have a dangerously disabling effect on a rider. Sufferers should be advised not to wear overtight jodphurs or breeches, and should certainly avoid tight-fitting boots. In cold weather, such riders will be better off wearing one pair of good-quality thermal socks, rather than risking the constriction of two pairs; they may also be well served by the jockey's ploy of wearing tights. Pupils at risk from cramp should not be expected to perform leg-stretching exercises, nor encouraged to ride (especially over jumps) with overlong leathers.

Asthma
Sufferers should not be asked to overexert themselves (this includes riding horses that are generally known to be hard work), and the instructor should take due care to avoid placing these riders in difficult or stressful situations. They should not be cajoled into assisting with grooming, filling haynets or other dusty tasks that might adversely affect their breathing. Consideration should also be given to the riding environment; some arenas can become very dusty and certain indoor schools can, in summer, be very hot and airless. Where such conditions exist, it may be advisable to make alternative arrangements.

Sight Defects
People with imperfect vision often think that they do not need to wear their spectacles when riding, perhaps

reasoning that leaving them off may prevent damage in the event of a fall. However, if their sight is significantly impaired, it really does require assistance for jumping and riding in the open. The obvious answer is to wear contact lenses, but some people cannot do so, while, if dust or grit gets beneath one at a critical moment, it can prove very disruptive. Spectacles with reinforced frames and shatter-proof plastic lenses may provide the solution. If the wearer is to do fast work in the open, it will be worthwhile having a pair made with fairly large lenses, as the wind can eddy around small ones and cause the eyes to water.

Impaired Hearing

Riders who are actually deaf would usually require the services of an instructor with specialist knowledge, but there are a number of people whose hearing – with or without augmentation – is impaired to some degree. This, of itself, will not affect their technical ability to ride (unless there is an associated condition affecting balance), but it can certainly hinder communication. The result of a pupil not hearing an instruction will usually be just mild inconvenience, but the potential exists for a more serious problem such as a collision in a group lesson or an accident – perhaps resulting from some lack of preparedness when riding out. Therefore, when teaching a pupil with im-paired hearing, an instructor must not be embarrassed about making himself heard; indeed, clear, precise, audible commands will assist *all* pupils. Where possible, it will help to face the pupil when speaking and/or to stand upwind in windy conditions. In potentially hazardous situations, the instructor should not be afraid to check that the pupil has heard a command; this can be done simply by enquiring 'All right there . . .?'

Obesity

In addition to resulting from pure overindulgence, obesity can also be related to medical conditions. When teaching a pupil who is significantly overweight, an instructor can first avoid potential difficulties for horse and rider by ensuring that a mounting block is provided. It should be borne in mind that extra flesh on thighs and buttocks will adversely affect the security and effectiveness of the seat, and being overweight will also reduce the pupil's stamina. Further, if the rider becomes out of balance with the horse, the effects will be greater than normal, so particular vigilance will be necessary in rising trot, canter and jumping. Where obesity *is* due solely to overindulgence, and the pupil is keen, it may be in order to explain (tactfully) the benefits of weight reduction and increased fitness!

Debilitating Conditions

Obviously, any pupils should be discouraged from riding while actually ill and so weakened that they will inevitably be ineffective and at risk. However, there are various conditions where a degree of debility may persist for some time, or even be permanent. In such cases, a keen rider may find that participating in a favourite sport provides at least a mental tonic, but there is an inherent possibility that such people may 'overdo it' and suddenly feel exhausted or faint.

With such clients, the ideal arrangement is to provide private, shortened periods of instruction or, if they are reasonably experienced, perhaps to ask them to act for a while as 'leading file' on a novice ride. These alternatives are preferable to being in a normal class lesson with their peers, when they may feel some obligation to participate for the whole period.

In general, an instructor should take care not to work

debilitated pupils too hard (the accent should be on movements requiring accuracy rather than physical effort), should make periodical enquiries as to how they are feeling, and allow opportunities for rest. Such pupils must not be encouraged to go for long rides out; indeed, if they ask to join such a ride, the request should be tactfully refused in the interests of all concerned.

Naturally, an instructor cannot readily give consideration to infirmities unless he or she is first aware of them. On occasion, an astute teacher may surmise that a problem exists because there is something about a pupil's riding style that does not 'add up', but, while such diagnostic ability is useful, it is better to have a full understanding of the problem from the start. In this matter, a teacher cannot and should not rely upon pupils to *volunteer* unsolicited information. Although some will do so, many will not, either through embarrassment, or because they simply do not appreciate the significance of their condition in the context of riding. Therefore, it is incumbent upon the instructor to enquire of new pupils whether they are suffering from *any* significant condition or injury, at the same time explaining the mutual benefits that may arise from such disclosure. At a commercial centre, where clients ride on a regular basis, it is good practice to make a written note of any long-term condition, in order that a client is not given an inappropriate horse or lesson by someone who is unaware of their situation. In addition to considerations of the pupil's welfare, such information may reduce the likelihood of insurance claims or litigation arising from an avoidable accident.

CHAPTER FOUR

Horses for Mature Riders

As we have already touched upon the need to ensure that riders with physical infirmities are not mounted on horses likely to aggravate their conditions, I would simply stress the need to exercise vigilance and common sense to ensure that this does not occur. It is also worth remembering the fact (sometimes ignored) that all novice riders will learn more easily, safely and comfortably on horses that, broadly speaking, are matched to their own physiques.

There is, however, another major consideration regarding horses for mature riders, and this relates to the old question of what constitutes a suitable horse for a novice. We can address this question first by making the analogy that no one with any sense would try to teach a learner driver in a car that kept stalling, jumped out of gear and had defective brakes, throttle and steering. In such circumstances, most sensible pupils would choose to give up before an accident befell them and, if one were sufficiently brave or audacious to continue, he or she would probably learn to drive in a fashion so bizarre as to be ineffective or dangerous in a roadworthy vehicle. Similarly, if one is trying to teach correct aid applications in riding, it follows that the pupil must have a horse that is capable of responding to them. This definition will exclude:

Riders will learn more early, safely and comfortably on horses matched to their own physiques

Horses too young to have been properly schooled and are consequentially unbalanced and unreliable.
Those too old or infirm to move and work properly.
Those that are lame or ill.

Those with serious long-standing physical defects and/or
conformation so poor that their movement is bad to
the point of being dangerous.

It should also be evident that the addition of abnormal
tack or gadgetry to an unsuitable horse *will not* render it
suitable for a novice rider; in fact, in this context, it is more
likely to exacerbate existing problems.

Ignoring such precepts carries the consequential risks
of accident, disillusionment and confusion and the best
scenario you could hope for in such circumstances is that
the pupil will learn to ride after a fashion, but with various
ingrained bad habits that will serve him or her ill on
correctly trained horses. To pursue this issue in the context
of the mature rider, it should be borne in mind that a
typical pupil will be reasonably intelligent, patient and
self-critical, willing to try to carry out instructions, and
prepared to accept constructive criticism. An instructor
cannot reasonably castigate such a pupil for ineffectiveness
or overriding if he or she is mounted on a horse to which
'textbook' aids are practically meaningless. There are three
specific reasons why this is so:

1) Criticisms of a novice pupil that are based on deficien-
   cies inherent in the horse distract attention from areas
   where genuine criticism is warranted, and create confusion in the pupil's mind. Thus, an instructor who
   ignores major defects in the horse and teaches as though
   they did not exist is, at best, misleading the pupil and, at
   worst, practicing deceit.

2) Such criticism is grossly unfair to a pupil, in that it
   effectively blames him or her for problems engendered
   or ignored by others. A philosophy such as 'squeeze,
   don't kick' may be strongly rooted in principle but,

addressed to a bemused, breathless, embarrassed novice, mounted on a horse with less animation than a pile of bricks, it represents little more than a gratuitous insult. It should be remembered that a novice pupil is paying to learn the basics, not to reschool the horse.

3) However ignorant of equestrian matters he or she may be initially, a pupil who patiently and persistently tries to follow instructions will expect more than failure and criticism. If these are all he or she gets, it will not be long before the pupil concludes that the instructor is a charlatan. Moreover, as in the driving analogy, there may be the occasional pupil who, through a mixture of commitment, frustration and provocation, determines to achieve results at any cost, with the consequence that he or she is launched on a path of rough or improper riding. If this person is not someone who would naturally wish to employ such techniques, he or she will have been done a great disservice.

It is, then, impractical to teach riding on unschooled horses, and this applies also to horses that have become terminally lazy or bored, and dead to the aids. The argument usually voiced by those riding schools who do employ hopeless plodders is that 'You can't put beginners on difficult, gassy horses'. This, though absolutely true, is no defence, because it presupposes that there is no equine middle ground between the brain-dead and the wild-eyed neurotic. Such supposition is, of course, arrant nonsense; a large proportion of horses, given correct schooling and management, are temperamentally suitable for novices under correct instruction, and there are numerous riding establishments that prove this point time and again.

Therefore, with the occasional exception of a pupil who

is especially nervous or virtually disabled, it makes sense to introduce pupils to riding on 'normal' horses, that is to say, those that display some degree of free forward movement and responsiveness. The basic philosophy should be 'This is a normal type of horse; this is how it moves, behaves and responds; and it is this you must learn to ride'. Given such a starting point, one can reasonably expect to teach pupils to ride along correct lines and to see evidence that the basic principles are being understood and put into practice. Once such a basis is established, pupils can be gradually educated in the ways of dealing with more difficult animals, and in the concept of teaching a horse rather than just sitting on it.

CHAPTER FIVE

Suitable Tack

Having discussed the suitability of horses for mature riders, this seems a logical moment to mention the need to ensure the suitability of the tack. When advising an owner-rider, this is pretty straightforward but when teaching at a commercial yard, where one has little day-to-day oversight of the tack room, constant vigilance is called for.

It should be self-evident that all tack should be in good condition and must fit, and be appropriate for, the horse upon which it is used. It is also important, however, that it 'fits' the rider. In the context of mature pupils who are riding at centres that cater for all age groups, this generally, but not necessarily, means that it should be big enough. Items for attention are:

Stirrup Irons
These should be big enough to ensure that the rider's feet cannot become wedged in them. (They should not, however, be so big that the feet can readily pass right through them. This is less likely to happen with mature people but, the way leathers are sometimes swapped around, it *could* happen to a small adult.)

Stirrup Leathers
These should be capable of adjustment to a length suitable

for the rider concerned; it is ridiculous to have a pupil's length of leg dictated by the available adjustment of the leathers.

Saddle

Bearing in mind that if a rider cannot sit correctly, he or she cannot ride correctly, the saddle should be a passable fit for the pupil. If riders are mounted on suitably sized horses this is likely to happen anyway, and the saddle should not fit the rider *at the expense* of the horse. However, it is conceivable that very tall, slim riders might be given a big horse on the grounds of height, and find themselves sliding around in a large saddle. It is also possible that a short, but rotund rider might be given a horse that is up to his or her weight but – through often being used for youngsters – has too small a saddle.

In addition to the matter of size, inappropriate or bad design should also be avoided. Saddles with a very high pommel can cause male riders to lose all interest in rising trot (and just about everything else!) and can also prove uncomfortable for ladies. Specialised jumping, showing and dressage saddles are (usually) fine for their intended purpose, but can prove a hindrance if employed for other disciplines. Old-fashioned hunting saddles, of the type with forward-cut panels and backward-sloping seat, are virtually useless for teaching correct posture as they encourage, or even provoke, the common novice fault of sitting on the back of the saddle with legs thrust forward.

As even an experienced rider will struggle to maintain a correct posture on a bad saddle, it should be borne in mind that it is grossly unfair to criticise a novice for postural errors induced by saddle design. Furthermore, telling a mature rider 'That saddle is awful, but you've still got to try

'Old-fashioned' saddles are virtually useless for teaching correct postures

to sit correctly' is likely to elicit a response along the lines of 'Why supply me with faulty equipment and then blame me for not being able to use it properly?'

Reins
Many reins used in commercial yards are too thin for anyone except small children. Adults with large hands, or

anyone a little arthritic, will find such reins extremely difficult to hold properly and, used for riding out in wet weather, they may be the cause of lost control. In all circumstances, gripping unduly hard in an effort to hold the reins will cause tension in the forearms and 'deaden' the rider's hands.

Reins that are too short, or unnecessarily long, are a potential danger to all riders.

Neckstrap

For very novice riders, and those having their first jumping lessons or rides out, it makes sense to provide neckstraps. It should be explained to pupils at a very early stage that the reins are not there to hold the rider on the horse and, indeed, are effectively incapable of performing that function. Therefore, should any situation arise in which a rider feels insecure, he or she should remove one hand from the reins, grasp the neckstrap and *sit up straight*. In this way, the pupil should avoid personal damage or damage to the horse, and also avoid upsetting the horse by hanging on to its mouth. If necessary, it can be pointed out that a neckstrap is a safety device rather than a badge of incompetence, often being provided for work riders in racing yards and not infrequently being employed (in the guise of a martingale) by those following hounds.

CHAPTER SIX

Advising on Riding Kit

One general difference between children and adults is that while the majority of children enjoy dressing up, the majority of adults do not. Furthermore, there is a strong tendency for adults to feel embarrassed in circumstances where 'they've got all the gear, but can't play the game'. Indeed, it would hardly be stretching the point to say that there is an unwritten convention that 'having all the gear' is considered a *mark* of proficiency, and novices avoid offending the convention by deliberately 'dressing down'.

While anthropologists would doubtless have a field day debating this issue, it is a major reason why very few adults will kit themselves out for riding until they have had a few lessons. The other, more pragmatic, reason is that new riding wear is not cheap, and many people will wish to confirm their long-term involvement in the sport before paying out. The consequence of these factors is that an instructor's role will often include giving initial advice on substitute riding wear, followed by encouragement to obtain the conventional items and advice on doing so.

The initial advice should, sensibly, be given *before* a pupil arrives for the first lesson. A dismissive 'Oh, you're wearing . . . they're no good for riding!' is a poor greeting, and likely to make the pupil irritated and defensive. On the other hand, a little time taken in advance will not only result in the pupil being more physically comfortable; the personal attention may also result in him or her feeling more welcome, thus helping to establish the basis of a good pupil/teacher relationship.

The essential item of riding wear is, of course, a hard hat that conforms to current BSI standards. Any decent teaching establishment will have a supply of these, and a new pupil can be assisted in finding one of correct fit upon arrival.

Where footwear is concerned, it should be noted that many beginners have no conception that certain types of shoes may be unsuitable, and it is particularly noticeable that an increasing number of people habitually wear 'trainers'. These, of course, offer very little protection to a foot trodden on by a horse and, despite their high-tech 'cushioning' construction, many have virtually flat soles. However, because of their sporting connotations, pupils may well turn up to ride in them if not otherwise advised. Traditional advice to novices without riding boots is to wear stout walking shoes but, while this remains sensible, the fact is that few people possess them nowadays. Many do, however, possess modern-type wellingtons – less cumbersome and closer fitting in the calf than the traditional type – and these may well suffice in the early stages. Beware of suggesting to ladies that they 'wear a shoe with a heel' and have them turn up in stilettos!

The question of what will serve as a substitute for breeches or jodphurs is very important in terms of rider comfort. In my opinion, nothing else is really satisfactory, but reasonably close-fitting 'moleskin' or corduroy trousers may serve. Ski pants have the virtues of being close-fitting and stretchy, but do not give much protection from chaffing, so a pupil wearing them would be well advised to fix large sticking plasters to the insides of his or her knees.

Where footwear is concerned, it should be noted that many beginners have no conception that certain types may be unsuitable

Failing all else, a pair of jeans will just about do if they are not too tight-fitting around hips and crutch. If they are too tight, they will render the rider virtually immobile – and there is a serious threat that they will emasculate a male rider as he attempts to mount. The other drawback with jeans (almost insignificant in comparison to the above) is that they tend to ruck up between the stirrup leathers and the insides of the knees, causing a good deal of pinching and chaffing.

43

To protect the upper body from cold or wet, many people nowadays wear bodywarmers or waxed jackets. Bodywarmers are generally fine for riding but it is preferable if jackets are short enough to prevent the rider from sitting on them or getting them caught behind the cantle. Although very long coats (such as Australian bush coats and traditional riding macs) circumvent such problems, they do make it difficult for an instructor to determine what a pupil is doing with seat and upper legs. Overgarments to be avoided are those made of plastic or nylon, which flap about and/or rustle.

In cold, wet weather, gloves are virtually essential. In the absence of purpose-made riding gloves, driving, or other relatively thin leather gloves will serve. Thermal under-gloves can be surprisingly useful for riding, but are unlikely to stand up to regular use. Traditional woollen gloves are of little use; when wet, they simply chill the rider's hands and their bulk in general will interfere with both grip and the feel of the reins, causing the rider to fumble.

During the course of their first few lessons, it is likely that pupils will begin to realise the limitations of substitute riding wear and start to think seriously about obtaining conventional kit. The probability is that they will then consult the instructor, who can explain the benefits and offer general guidance.

While instructors will doubtless draw on their own experiences of riding wear, there are certain points that should be stressed if pupils are to derive maximum benefit from their kit:

Hard Hats
It is very important that riders buy *new* hats, which should conform to current BSI standards (4472 or 6473). While

44

emphasis is rightly put upon a hat being a good fit for safety reasons, it is also important, in terms of comfort, that it is the right *shape* for the wearer's head. Many 4472 'crash hats' seem to be rather oval in section, which can result in them being plenty big enough from back to front, but rather tight around the temples. This can make them very uncomfortable and quite headache-inducing if worn for long periods. It is, therefore, worth a rider's time shopping around and trying different makes of hat to ensure comfort as well as safety.

Boots
Although they should be close-fitting around both foot and calf, boots should not be too tight, as this will make them uncomfortable to walk in, will create difficulty in wearing thick socks in cold weather and, most seriously, may induce cramp – a most dangerous and undesirable condition for a rider.

Furthermore, should a rider have the misfortune to suffer an injury to foot or ankle, tight boots – made tighter by any swelling – can be painful, difficult and even expensive to remove if they need to be cut off.

Pupils should, generally, be steered away from cheap, unlined rubber boots, which rarely fit well, wear out quickly and are unpleasant to wear in both hot and cold weather. Much better quality lined rubber boots are available, and many have the benefit of being produced in various calf sizes. These are still subject to drawbacks, however; one manufacturer seems to make only narrow foot widths, and another makes all sizes over-generous around ankle and instep, which can cause the boots to slip down at the heels if the wearer rides without stirrups. However, by shopping around, it is likely that most people will be able to find serviceable rubber boots of reasonable quality, and they have the benefits of being virtually maintenance-free, waterproof and much cheaper than leather. None the less, for the rider who can afford them, the advantages of leather boots are that, correctly fitted, they are the most comfortable boots, provide the best protection and support and, properly cared for, will last for ages. If money is no object, a pupil seeking leather boots is best directed to a specialist manufacturer, while the rather less well-off may have the good fortune to find a suitable pair of 'seconds', or actual secondhand boots, at a favourable price. Jodphur boots may be cheaper than full-length boots, but they give no protection against the pinching of the leathers and few people over the age of ten look at all distinguished in them.

Breeches/Jodphurs

In the past, adult resistance to 'dressing up' was perhaps most commonly manifested in feelings of self-consciousness about wearing breeches or jodphurs, especially beyond the confines of the riding school. The current availability of various colours and new materials, such as stretch denim, seems to have reduced the impact of this factor; colours such as black and navy, and garments that are essentially 'stretch jeans', are perhaps less obtrusive than the traditional fawn or cream, and many adults seem more socially comfortable in the new garments. Indeed, many riders now wear relatively inexpensive coloured breeches for 'everyday' riding, and keep a traditional pair for showing or competing.

Regardless of the style preferred, breeches and jodphurs must be suitable for their purpose; although close-fitting, they should not be too tight behind the knees, or around

Jodphur boots: few people over the age of 10 look at all
distinguished in them

hips and buttocks. Useful tests for purchasers are that they
should be able to perform a dismounted 'rising trot'
without restriction, and adopt a jockey-style crouch in
comfort. My own personal tip is that people who intend to
ride out extensively should also look for a garment with
zipped pockets.

The other item of kit to mention is the whip. It is highly
unlikely that a newcomer to riding will arrive with a whip;
indeed, many novices are reluctant to carry one. The
reasons for this are first that it has connotations with

punishment (quite laudably, they do not wish to be considered as people who would treat horses harshly) and second, they reason that carrying a whip presupposes that a rider is sufficiently experienced to make accurate judgements about when to use it, and thus it would be pretentious of them to do so. A third objection, sometimes voiced, is that a whip will 'clutter up the hands' and generally get in the way.

However, while there is no point in a rider carrying a whip while being introduced to riding on the lunge, there are grounds for starting to carry one, and understanding its uses, at quite an early stage. It is certainly important for a rider to understand that the whip is not primarily an instrument of punishment but a useful, and sometimes quite subtle, adjunct to the natural aids. Knowing this, and learning to use the whip properly, can help to prevent a rider from learning the bad habit of giving incessant 'nagging' leg aids, and generally 'working too hard'. Carrying, changing over and using a whip also contribute towards improving co-ordination and manual dexterity and, furthermore, whips can be employed in exercises to illustrate the stillness (or otherwise) of the hands and upper body.

While most riding establishments have an assortment of whips available for loan, these tend to be old, ruined and of poor design. For the few pounds it will cost, it is well worthwhile riders buying their own. For novices, a standard 76 cm whip is preferable to a schooling whip; although many of the latter are too short for their purpose, they are still long enough for a novice to find them cumbersome and, until a rider has a secure posture and full control of his or her hands, there is the risk of pulling the horse in the mouth when applying a schooling whip.

When buying a whip, consideration should be given to the fact that it is a tool with a purpose, and must therefore suit that purpose. To this end, it should be properly balanced and have a handle thick enough to ensure that the rider's hand does not become tense trying to grip it. There should also be a significant knob at the top to make it harder to drop, but there should not be a wrist loop, because this would cause it to get snagged in anything and everything, and induce incessant fumbling on the part of its carrier.

CHAPTER SEVEN

Preliminaries to Riding

Establishing Familiarity with Horses

Until quite recent times, it was probable that most people had experienced at least a rudimentary contact with horses. Nowadays, however, an instructor may quite frequently be confronted with adult pupils who, to all intents and purposes, are completely unfamiliar with them. In some cases, while they will have a general 'liking' for horses, they may actually confess to being a little frightened of them. Although such terminology can be something of a self-effacing exaggeration (and they are unlikely to be truly phobic), it is quite possible that these people do, at least, have an instinctive wariness of the unknown. This attitude is not necessarily contradictory to their liking of horses; it is quite possible for someone to think of horses as being beautiful, noble, exciting and so forth but to find, at close quarters, that a horse remains much the largest animal they have ever had contact with and they may feel (quite justifiably) that if one did bite, kick or behave unpredictably, the result could be distinctly unpleasant. In other cases, of course, people will be completely at ease in the presence of a horse but may still have as little, or less, idea of 'what makes it tick' as their more diffident companions.

Where such unfamiliarity exists, it will be evident that there are distinct advantages in increasing pupils' basic confidence and understanding *before* expecting them to sit

'Has it got fuel injection and power steering?'! Nowadays, an instructor may quite frequently be confronted with people who, to all intents and purposes, are completely unfamiliar with horses

on horses and start trying to control them. The argument that this cannot be done because 'pupils have paid to ride and want to get on with it' not only shows a lack of understanding of the above, but also misses the point that an instructor in any sport is bound to spend a little time introducing pupils to their 'equipment' and the principles of the 'game'. It also ignores the fact that, at many commercial

51

yards, lessons are arranged to continue for longer periods than an unfit beginner can gainfully spend in the saddle – a point we shall discuss further in due course.

Obviously, there is a limit to what can be done at the start of a first lesson, but anything that enhances confidence before pupils mount for the first time must be a bonus. To this end, an instructor can take pupils into the box of an amenable horse and demonstrate basic techniques for approaching and handling. Although any techniques demonstrated should be correct and safe, precisely what is done is not especially important; the primary objective at this stage being simply to get pupils close to, and preferably in physical contact with, a horse. This process of building up confidence and familiarity should be a continual one, progressing in time to (supervised) grooming, tacking up and so forth, and to establishing an interest in stable management. In the long term, through helping pupils to understand more about horses, this procedure is bound to help their actual riding, and may prove invaluable experience for those who go on to own or share a horse.

Mounting and Dismounting
Provided that a rider is reasonably able-bodied and the horse is well mannered and not too big, mounting should be a simple process, painless to both parties. However, if one considers the number of able-bodied, relatively experienced riders who habitually make a complete pig's breakfast of the operation, it will be apparent that with less agile, unfit beginners there is the distinct possibility of the mental or physical upset of both horse and rider if due care is not taken by the instructor. It will also be apparent that a correct grounding is necessary for all pupils, regardless of their physical condition, in order that they should not develop

bad habits. Further to this, it should be remembered that a rider is relatively vulnerable while in the act of mounting, and sloppy, careless practices can open the way for an unexpected accident.

Therefore, although it will be in a pupil's interest if he or she can learn, in due course, to mount unaided from either side of the horse, there should be no initial emphasis on mounting as being an end in itself, as this will just encourage pupils to get up anyhow. Instead, an instructor should take the attitude that the whole purpose of mounting is to arrive in the saddle with the minimum of fuss, effort or discomfort for horse or rider. To this end, it makes sense to employ a safe, solid mounting block for all beginners, and to give each pupil personal supervision. While a mounting block will doubtless prevent much unwanted and possibly embarrassing clambering, the instructor can explain that its purposes go beyond simply being a 'step' for the rider; it also helps to reduce strain on saddlery and, by minimising discomfort and loss of balance in the horse, makes it less likely that it will learn to fidget while being mounted.

When supervising beginners, it is important that even though the instructor has checked the tack and a mounting block is employed, each pupil is specifically taught to check his or her own girth, in order that the habit becomes quickly ingrained.

At the stage where pupils are taught to mount from the ground, it is important to emphasise that they should stand close to the horse with their right leg (when mounting from the nearside) well 'underneath' them, and use this leg to *spring* up. Most riders who experience difficulty mounting do so because they fail to use the right leg enough – instead, they try to climb into the saddle by putting excessive pressure into the left stirrup and hauling on the cantle.

Correct instruction at an early stage can prevent a great deal of discomfort to horse and rider, and increase the life of saddlery.

Dismounting, cleanly, conventionally and successfully is dependent upon the rider swinging his or her legs back and up sufficiently for the right leg to clear the horse's quarters and the cantle of the saddle. If the rider does not do this, he or she will catch a leg and slip or topple off in a heap. Most beginners, especially the stiff, unfit or diffident, will fail to clear the quarters/cantle unless they have been specifically told of the need to do so, and their problems may be exacerbated by a fear that swinging their legs back too energetically will result in diving head first over the horse's shoulder.

The best way to alleviate such fears, and demonstrate the amount of movement required to dismount cleanly, is to demonstrate it oneself or, better still, to have it demonstrated by a more experienced mature pupil, should one be available. However, regardless of how much care is taken over an instructor's explanations, dismounting is something riders must do for themselves and it will either be done smoothly or with considerable loss of balance. It makes sense, therefore, if the instructor is close at hand for the pupil's first couple of attempts, in order to give any assistance that may be necessary.

Incidentally, it is, or once was, apparently the policy in certain cavalry regiments to mount and dismount 'by numbers' – that is to say, in a series of separate movements rather than one flowing one. When dismounting in this manner, the rider only quit his offside stirrup initially, and used the nearside one as a 'step' down. Although this may seem superficially attractive for a less agile rider, dismounting in this manner requires a relatively long pause with most of the weight in one stirrup. As well as putting unnecessary strain on the tack (and the rider at the mercy of any failure thereof), this also puts the rider in potential difficulty or danger if, through habit, he or she eventually employs this method on a flighty, fidegety or frightened horse. Many novices will attempt to dismount in this way, especially if they have seen too many Western movies. It is very dangerous with 'English' tack and must not be allowed.

CHAPTER EIGHT

First and Early Lessons

Introduction Via the Lunge

It has long been acknowledged that the ideal way of introducing a pupil to riding is on the lunge. Although, in Britain, it is probable that the majority still do not begin this way, the advantages are many.

From a technical viewpoint, working on the lunge frees a rider from the basic concerns of control, and allows concentration upon posture, increasing depth of seat, and becoming familiar with the horse's movement.

Freeing a beginner from the problems of control is very useful: instinctively, along with 'staying on top', rudimentary control will be his or her main concern and preoccupation with it can clutter the mind, actually inhibiting the absorbtion of instructions aimed at enhancing security and control. (This is a paradox of teaching that all instructors should be aware of. Most of us, if we are honest, can recall times when we have felt like saying, 'Shut up, I'm trying to ride' to someone whose intention it is to help us do just that. This is why – providing the pupil is not going to be endangered – it is often better to explain what is required before starting an exercise and then discuss it afterwards, keeping comment to a minimum while it is in progress.)

Another good reason for freeing beginners from control is that, through an instinctive desire for 'control at any price', they may start to develop bad habits (for example, incorrect rein aids) that will not only need to be eradicated later, but which may actually compound their problems of the moment.

Allowing full concentration upon correct posture and depth of seat are factors that are vastly and inexcusably underrated; in addition to increasing a pupil's security greatly, the corollaries of a still upper body and hands and lack of gripping with the legs will permit far more correct and effective aid applications. Indeed, many faults for which novice riders are criticised are inevitable *symptoms* of incorrect posture, and will never be eradicated until the underlying problem is solved. In other words, reasonably correct posture is a fundamental prerequisite without which little meaningful progress can be made.

Regarding familiarity with the horse's movement, this, at the most basic level, can simply refer to riders getting used to the fact that there is a living creature moving beneath them. The significance of this can be easily overlooked by someone who has been riding for many years, but it is worth remembering that the initial experience can be entirely novel – especially for an adult. Whereas children will often be used to the significant movement of various conveyances (swings, fairground rides, roller skates, etc.) an adult's recent experience may be limited to the motion of a car cushioned by modern suspension. Thus the initial movement – or, indeed, any unexpected movement – of the horse may be completely unlike anything to which they are accustomed, and the instinctive reaction to *unaccustomed* movement is to grab hold of something. If present, that something is likely to be the reins, and this is another good reason for starting a pupil on the lunge where he or she can, if necessary, hold on to a neckstrap or saddle arch, but not the horse's mouth. Furthermore, although a pupil will certainly experience the horse's movement whether on the lunge or not, he or she is likely to gain a more useful 'feel' of correct movement if it is being produced and regulated by the instructor.

After simply experiencing the sensation of movement, the next stage entails the first steps towards learning how to absorb it, a process inextricably linked to work on seat and posture. Again, it will initially be easier for the pupil if he or she does not also have to create and regulate the movement – the truth of this can be seen in the alternative of novices struggling to learn to rise at a trot that they cannot regulate, precisely because they cannot yet absorb it. Of course, the process of learning to absorb movement (and, later, the uses of the seat as an aid to regulation) will continue long after a pupil is first 'let off' the lunge, but this is no reason not to give a sound introduction, and there is always value in returning periodically to the lunge when concentrating on this aspect of riding.

From the pupil's point of view, then, the main advantage of having the first few lessons on the lunge lies in the technical progress that can be made, and this will be reinforced by the benefits accruing from individual attention and intensive instruction. Further to this, any pupil who is sufficiently serious to look beyond simply 'buying time on a horse' should be readily persuaded that (despite apparent price differences) this represents better value for money than starting with group lessons, even if the latter are small and well conducted.

The essential value of introductory lunge lessons is, however, directly dependent upon their quality and content. This, of course, applies to all lessons, but it is worth stressing because there is a tendency, in some quarters, to assume that there is inherent virtue in the mere act of lungeing. This is not, in fact, the case; indeed, just as a good lunge lesson represents exceptionally good value, so a bad one represents exceptionally bad value. The elements that contribute towards good and bad lessons are:

Good	Bad
A separate, enclosed lungeing area, ideally about 20 m square.	Lungeing in an area being used by other riders or, worse still, a field with loose horses! (It should be remembered that if a horse *does* get distracted or startled while being lunged, it will be much harder to control than if it were being ridden free by someone experienced. By the time control is regained, the learner on the lunge may have had an unpleasant, if not dangerous, experience.)
A sound, even surface.	A treacherous surface. If a horse does fall while being lunged, it usually goes down suddenly and hard. The repercussions for the rider are obvious.
Absence of any extraneous material that might distract the horse, trip the instructor, snag the lunge line.	Presence of any such material.
A comfortable, even-gaited horse of good temperament, who is used to lunge work and shows willing obedience, so that the instructor can concentrate on the pupil rather than the horse.	An uncomfortable horse with poor gaits, especially one that may trip itself up through 'plaiting'. A horse of uncertain temperament. A horse unused to lunge work.

Good	Bad
	A lazy horse that dissipates the instructor's thoughts and energies.
Working the horse on a circle large enough to permit a good balance and rhythm, but not so large that the instructor forfeits full control, or makes the pupil feel 'remote'.	Working on an inappropriate circle.
Good lungeing technique.	Poor lungeing technique.

Because of the intensity of working on the lunge, the actual period of lungeing should not exceed twenty minutes. If the pupil is relatively unfit or stiff, there should also be short breaks beyond those that would normally arise when changing the rein. Any breaks should be usefully filled with discussion and explanation. Assuming that the standard lesson time is half an hour, the few minutes at the end of the lungeing session can be used to start introducing the pupil to basic aspects of riding off the lunge. As pupils progress at different rates, and experience different problems, the precise content of both the lunge lessons and the ensuing instruction must be at the instructor's discretion. However, by way of example, the first few minutes off the lunge might entail the instructor leading the horse while introducing the pupil to the principles of holding and using the reins. Later sessions might allow the pupil to practise a little of what has been learnt on the lunge, free of a lungeline or leadrope, with reins and without side reins. It is at this juncture that the further advantages of a reasonably small, enclosed arena and suitable horse will become apparent in

A treacherous surface

that the horse, having just worked on the lunge, is likely to circle quite readily around the instructor and remain obedient to voice commands, should they prove necessary.

61

Transition to Group Lessons

After a few such lessons, a pupil should have reached a stage at which he or she can gainfully join a small group lesson with others of similar experience. There may, occasionally, be pupils who are prepared to continue paying for private lessons and perhaps, for various reasons, would prefer to do so. Despite the advantages of this, there is also a drawback, which is that these people will not gain any experience of riding in company. Although in exceptional circumstances (such as an actor's intensive preparation for a role) this may not be relevant, it is usually very much so, as most riders – inevitably and mainly intentionally – spend a considerable amount of their riding time in company. This being the case, there are two important reasons why all pupils should be encouraged to spend at least some of their time in group lessons. These are:

1) In order to get used to controlling a horse that is under the influence of others nearby. At this stage, such influences may be manifest by those little 'tricks' beloved of crafty old school horses: reluctance to pass the ride, the magnetic attraction of the rear file, the tendency to follow if the horse in front executes a turn, and so on. (Obviously, if horses are to be deemed suitable for novice riders, such quirks must not be evident to nuisance level, but to assume their total absence would be optimistic in the extreme.) The sooner pupils can become aware of the potential disparities in behaviour between a horse alone and in company, the sooner they can start thinking of adjusting their aid applications as necessary to remain effective. An early introduction along these lines will prevent the pupils acquiring false perspectives of their progress, or falling into the trap of automatically blaming a horse for exhibiting behavioural

differences in varied circumstances or surroundings. The benefits of such understanding will become increasingly evident as they progress, for example, to riding out in company.

2) To develop the idea of a rider's *responsibility* for controlling his or her horse – in other words, to discourage any acceptance on the rider's part that he or she is a passenger, and to promote the idea that *the rider* must ensure that the horse does not barge into, 'carve up' or otherwise impede others. Again, the sooner pupils understand this principle the better; it will promote thoughtful and effective riding, thereby improving safety in the arena, and will also stand them in good stead when they reach the stage of riding on roads, in places where pedestrians are present, and in generally crowded situations.

Obviously, as novice riders cannot invariably be expected to exercise full control, an instructor must ensure, by general good practice, that he or she does not induce situations that will put too great an onus on them. What we are concerned with is not some 'baptism of fire', but simply promoting an awareness that responsibility for control is part of the reality of riding. An analogy to this is that it is perfectly sensible for people starting driving lessons to learn the basics of control in an environment where any error will threaten neither themselves nor any other party. However, if their lessons are to be of any practical value they must, in due course, be introduced gently to the realities of employing these controls in the context of other road users.

Basic Elements of Early Group Lessons
CLASS SIZE
It is essential that class size is such that an instructor

proper attention both to the class as a whole and to individual pupils. The first reason for this is so that the teacher can do all within his or her power to ensure safety; the second reason is so that each pupil may receive sufficient individual input to maintain a good rate of progress – any deficiency in this respect being especially obvious to pupils who have, hitherto, made good progress on the lunge.

While appreciating the need for both freelance instructors and riding establishments to be commercially successful, I would suggest that those intending to give 'value for money' should consider six riders to be a practical maximum in a novice lesson and, ideally, that classes should be smaller than this. One way to achieve this, while keeping up the number of 'clients per hour', is to offer beginners lessons of less than an hour's duration – an idea we shall consider shortly.

Those establishments that habitually put excessive numbers of clients in lessons cannot claim, in any meaningful sense, to be offering tuition, and presumably have little or no interest in their pupils' progress.

LESSON DURATION
At an early stage, lessons of an hour's duration may be too long for a significant proportion of mature pupils. By the latter stages of such a lesson, they may really have had enough, and be secretly counting the minutes to the end. Thus, not only will tiredness/soreness/aches reduce their physical efficiency, they will also be having a distracting effect, leading to loss of concentration. There is no doubt that such pupils will derive more benefit from two half-hourly lessons a week than from one full hour, if such a programme can be arranged to the convenience of themselves and the establishment where they are learning. The

corollary to this is that if pupils *do* have half-hour lessons, these should be as full as possible of actual instruction; it is not fair to spend half the lesson time getting pupils mounted, and then have prolonged 'rests' while the instructor gives a fence by fence account of 'How I won the local hunter trial'. Obviously, given such a regime, pupil interest in stable management will have to be fostered at a time that does not encroach upon the riding lesson.

If, however, an instructor is working at a commercial yard that is irrevocably geared up for hourly sessions, he or she may face the task of avoiding pupil fatigue without wasting their time. In such circumstances it can make good sense to suggest that pupils pursue the process of increasing their understanding of horses, and to offer to spend the first few minutes of each lesson on a cohesive programme of stable management, with emphasis on those areas that involve pupils in actually handling suitable horses.

It may also be useful to allocate a specified time – five minutes or so – at the end of each lesson for a proper discussion about what has taken place – an arrangement that is more useful, and more likely to stimulate response, than the common, hurried 'Any questions? – No – right, let's put the horses away'. Another advantage of this arrangement is that it allows time to refer back to any question asked during the lesson, which, while of general interest, was not strictly relevant to the moment at which it was raised. To use time in such ways will, of course, require willing acceptance by the pupils, but there is a good prospect that mature people will be persuaded of the benefits of a lesson that increases all-round knowledge rather than one that force-feeds technical skills to the point of exhaustion.

Further to this topic of lesson duration there have, at various times, been establishments that worked on the basis of 45-minute lessons, each starting on the hour and ending at a quarter to. This, in theory, is a good idea, because it gives both stables and pupils a little 'breathing space' and room for manouevre, and should prevent lessons from running late. With the 'compromise' in lesson time, this arrangement should be particularly suitable for both mature riders and children. Unfortunately, however, the idea does not seem to have become popular: this may be due in part to a feeling by riding establishments that the intervals are 'dead time' for which they could have charged, and a suspicion on the part of clients that any financial adjustments were not sufficient to prevent their being 'shortchanged'. Nevertheless, having seen the pressure on staff, erosion of lesson time and cumulative late running that affect many busy riding schools, one wonders whether this alternative arrangement might not, on balance, be beneficial. It would certainly seem worth consideration by freelance instructors who have to commute between pupils, and who risk arriving late at their next lesson after killing time with a pupil who has really run out of steam before the end of a full hour's private instruction.

LEADING FILE

For the first few group lessons it is definitely helpful to both teacher and pupils to have a somewhat more experienced rider as leading file. This can be a useful role for a rider who is returning to riding after a long absence or is recovering from illness. Ideally, it is perhaps better not to have a *very* experienced person in this role, on the dual basis that he or she may not derive much benefit from it, while simultaneously overaweing the other pupils and perhaps making them feel embarrassed about their own efforts. In most cases, however, an instructor will not have much choice in this matter, and such a person would certainly be preferable to another who had an active inclination to show off.

After the first few lessons it is good practice, as far as possible, to give all pupils an equal turn in taking leading file, the chief constraint being the relative size and stride length of the horses employed. Further to this, although much early work will be performed 'as a ride', it is better from the viewpoint of safety if riders are not expected to work in too close an order. One advantage of small groups is that pupils can be asked to keep two horses' length apart, which requires both a little more control and permits a little more room for manoeuvre should a problem arise.

CONTENT

In addition to attention to posture and basic aid applications, this should include plenty of work on basic transitions and the accurate riding of simple figures. Such exercises consolidate control and thus improve confidence and may also, by keeping pupils mentally occupied, help to alleviate any tension, nervousness or preoccupation with minutiae.

General instructional points to bear in mind are:

1) When riding transitions in the early stages, pupils will be asked more of a 'question', and thus become more effective, if they ride downward transitions one at a time from the rear of the ride, and upward transitions one at a time from the front. The other advantage of this is that it lessens the possibility of a collision resulting from the whole ride being asked to perform a transition in unison, and certain elements failing to do so (although such exercises can have value once pupils have become more proficient).

2) With figure work it is, again, beneficial if pupils are sometimes asked to perform exercises individually so that the ride does not develop into a game of follow my leader, with horses following on anyhow and cutting corners while their riders adopt an overpassive role.

Further to this, as pupils progress, there will be value in spending some time on basic formation riding; it helps riders to be aware of what is going on around them, to ride accurately, and to regulate their horses' rhythm. However, an instructor should never become so preoccupied with drill riding that he or she places more importance on a rider's relative position in the formation than on whether it was achieved or sustained by correct technique.

Basic Commands and Geometry of the Arena

If pupils are to perform as above, they will need an early introduction to the traditional commands and figures of the riding arena. It is easy for somebody totally familiar with these to forget that, for novice pupils, these terms may be virtually meaningless, but lack of explanation can result in confusion and disruption.

Like most specialised activities, riding has its own jargon, and it is important to remember that its only value is as a convenient 'shorthand'. It is pretentious and condescending to explain jargon terms in a manner that suggests to pupils that they are being indoctrinated in the mysteries of some secret society – a mature pupil will not want a metaphorical pat on the head for guessing what 'go large' means.

Command phrases that should be explained before being employed include:

the outside track	change the rein
the inside track	go large
the outside leg/rein	form a ride
the inside leg/rein	the whole ride
on the left rein	leading file
on the right rein	rear file
	open order

(Note that before any work is done in open order, it is essential to explain the convention of riders working on different reins passing left shoulder to left shoulder.)

As movements are specified by reference to the arena markers, it will help both pupils and instructor if the former can learn the juxtaposition of the markers as soon as possible. Many people, if left to their own devices, will take ages to do this, so it is worth stressing the relevance and providing a little assistance. Mnemonics such as 'All King Edward's Horses Can Manage Big Fences' (A, K, E, H, C, M, B, F) can help, but are less useful in movements where the sequence is broken, for example, crossing a diagonal (HF, etc.). It may therefore help if an instructor keeps a supply of diagrams of a standard arena to hand out to novice pupils, so that they can peruse them at convenient moments between lessons. It can also be instructive, on two fronts, if exercises performed individually occasionally include some less common routes around the arena. If, for example, the exercise is for leading file only to trot to the rear of the ride, the ride might be halted at C, and the prescribed route be MXAFEH. This will not only focus the rider's attention on where he or she is going, but will also require more accurate riding than simply going large to the rear.

In addition to teaching the relative 'geography' of the arena, an instructor must ensure that pupils understand the basic geometry of movements. In this respect, it should be

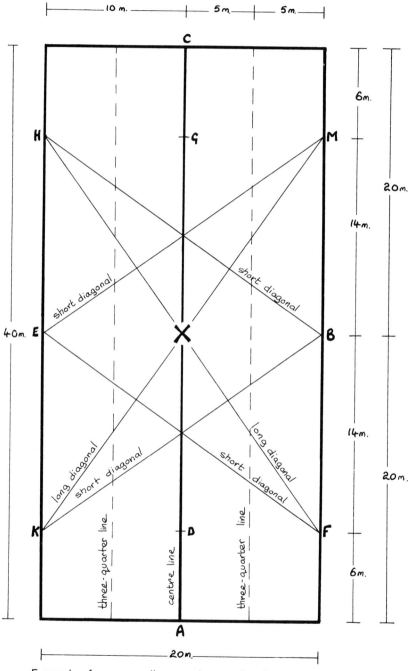

Example of an arena diagram that can be given to novice pupils

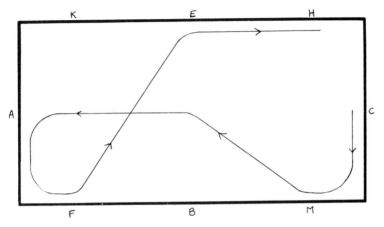

Example of a route 'to the rear of the ride', designed to improve pupils' familiarity with arena markers and to promote thoughtful, accurate riding

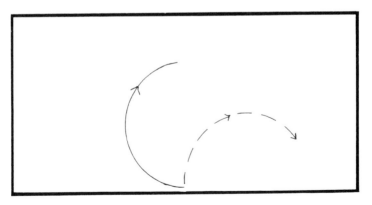

Riding a half-circle: the dotted line is an example of a common pupil misconception and one that should be guarded against

noted that many intelligent adults seem to have no concept of geometry whatsoever, and it may be necessary to spell out basics such as, in a 40 × 20 m arena, a 20 m circle from A or C must touch X. Such information should, of course, be imparted with a reasonable degree of tact, so that one might say, 'The exercise will be to ride a 20 m circle left from C, so be sure to touch the outside track halfway between the first corner and E, ride through X and touch the outside track halfway between B and the next corner . . . and don't ride too deeply into the corners.'

If it is necessary, as it is in many cases, to make instructions this precise, it will be apparent that proper definitions must be given for all figures (it sometimes helps to walk them oneself), and that apparent anomalies must be explained. For example:

'Quarter markers' are *not* a quarter of the way down the arena, but 6 m from the corners.

'Long diagonals' are ridden from quarter marker to quarter marker, not from corner to corner (which would be correct in geometrical terms).

In riding, it is accepted that the size of a circle is defined by reference to its diameter.

The command 'From (a named marker) ride a x m half circle (l/r)' means proceed as though to ride a full circle from that marker, but only go halfway. It does not mean 'Haul the horse off the track at an acute angle and try to regain the track x m behind where you started from.' (This may sound far-fetched, but I have seen novice riders attempt it.)

It is especially important that the precise nature of various loops and serpentines is explained in advance – it should be borne in mind that outside its riding context the word 'serpentine' means nothing more specific than 'snakelike'.

Further to the twin subjects of arena markers and correct figure work, special care must be exercised when teaching in a non-standard arena, where markers are located in what can, at best, be approximate positions. While the markers will still be useful when giving directions, it will be necessary to define precisely what is meant by certain commands. If, for example, an arena is 30 m wide, one should not tell a pupil to 'Ride a 20 m circle from B', and then remonstrate with them if they do not touch the outside track at E. If your intention was for them to do this, the command should have been 'From B, ride a circle the whole width of the school'. It is especially confusing for pupils with competitive ambitions to learn movements in a non-standard arena if those movements are based on the instructor's assumption that the arena *is* of standard size.

Introduction Without Lunge Lessons
The converse of persuading pupils of the value of group lessons lies in the problems that must be faced when they are taught in groups from the start. Ideals aside, it is a fact that many riding establishments do not have a regular policy of introducing beginners on the lunge and many instructors, whether freelance or retained, will have to deal with this scenario. For the considerate instructor, the underlying drawback to this is effectively insurmountable, in that, however skilful he or she is, this instructor will never be able to give a beginner in a group the same 'value' that could be offered via an introduction on the lunge. However, if a job is worth doing, it is worth doing as well as possible, and

the way to achieve this is through minimising the inherent disadvantages.

In the first place, a class for absolute beginners *must* be reasonably small. I have already touched on the question of class size, but it is worth emphasising that no instructor can give a safe, useful lesson to a large group of complete beginners. If such is expected, it can be considered evidence that the stable proprietor has very little understanding of his or her business and, under such circumstances, the job is probably *not* worth doing at all.

Second, horses used for beginners in group lessons *must* be fitted with neckstraps, the purpose of which should be explained at the start of the first lesson, and the instructor must stress – and repeat as necessary – that the reins are not for hanging on by. Stressing that the seat must be independent of the reins is a fundamental requirement when teaching beginners off the lunge and, indeed, mirrors what they would learn more readily if they had had the advantage of lunge lessons.

Third, a major disadvantage of teaching in this way is that, for the minimum of the first couple of lessons, the majority of pupils will need to be led or, at least, have someone walking at their horses' heads. This makes considerable demands on a yard's staff, and a consequence is the tendency to employ any available youngsters for the purpose. This provides the potential for two drawbacks:

1) Such 'leaders' have a tendency to usurp the instructor's role, giving (often superfluous and inaccurate) information about the horses and how to ride them, and generally distracting the pupils' attention. Although inevitably well intentioned, such behaviour can be a significant nuisance for both teacher and pupil. It can, however, be avoided by emphasising to those doing the

leading (politely, and not in the presence of the pupils) that it would be appreciated if they were to confine their role to leading alone, and not talking.

2) Being led by a youngster may, to some adults, be a rather demeaning introduction. This is best minimised by explaining to all pupils that the initial emphasis is simply on becoming used to being on horseback, getting comfortable, establishing basic posture and receiving an explanation of the basic aids, and that this is easier if they do not also have to assume immediate full control. (This, again, mirrors what would take place in early lunge lessons, and is not contrary to the concept of teaching responsibility for control, which is introduced once pupils have reached a stage at which they can be reasonably expected to implement it.)

Following on from this, provision of a suitable leading file is perhaps even more crucial for pupils learning in this way than for those who have had the prior benefit of lunge lessons.

Another general disadvantage of starting beginners in a group is that people inevitably learn at different rates. Although this is a continuing factor with which all teachers of groups have to contend, its effect is greatest in the early stages. The reasons for this is that, in the first instance, some people are inherently quicker 'starters' than others, so that, in the course of the first few lessons, it is quite possible that one pupil may make much more rapid progress than another. In the longer term, such differentials tend to decrease but even when they do not, once pupils have been riding for a certain time, it is usually possible to accommo-date different abilities by placing more or less advanced pupils in appropriate classes. When introducing riders via the lunge, the problem can be similarly circumvented by keeping them to individual lessons until a certain standard is achieved.

When pupils start in groups, however, even the most precocious are still, effectively, 'beginners', and an instructor will need to exercise considerable skill and discretion to ensure that he or she neither holds back the faster learners nor ignores those who are slower – both damaging errors when pupils are at such a formative stage. This task may become a little easier if the instructor remembers that, generally speaking, mature pupils will understand and accept that they will learn at different rates, and it is unlikely that they will have any particular desire to compete with their peers, or be resentful of another's progress. Therefore, if the instructor can subtly establish a mutual acknowledgement of the different needs and progress of the pupils, he or she will be free, as far as is practical, to deal with them as a collection of individuals, rather than as an amorphous body whose elements need to be chivvied or restrained in order to comply with some abstract 'norm' of progress.

From a technical viewpoint, one early major issue that confronts anyone instructing a group of beginners is the teaching of trot. Usually, pupils introduced to this gait off the lunge are effectively encouraged to *avoid* the horse's movement by being taught rising trot first. Although this may be a short-term expedient (and occasionally necessary, as in the case of a pupil with severe lower back trouble), it often promotes early errors in the trot itself – rising from the stirrups, rising too high and getting out of balance, related ineffectiveness of the leg aids. It also creates a hiccup in the learning process in that, just when pupils need to develop some depth of seat and learn to absorb movement, they are being taught the opposite. In the context of teaching mature pupils, with the possible ramifications of

Early errors in rising trot

general stiffness and lack of fitness, the temptation for instructors to teach this way are perhaps increased but, assuming that they wish their pupils to attain a reasonable standard, doing so is only evading the issue. In order to achieve such a standard, pupils will have to learn to sit to the trot at some stage, and there are good reasons for their doing so sooner rather than later. These are, first, that even if it proves initially difficult, attempting to do so, and in due course succeeding, will help to improve posture and seat; second, that it will help to prevent the development of bad habits; third, that it will give pupils time to consolidate the sitting trot before they attempt to canter. The importance of this last point will become obvious through the observation of pupils who are encouraged to attempt canter before they can sit reasonably to the trot; they can neither ride the transitions to or from canter properly, nor sit the gait itself, and this is often the cause of first falls.

(It should be noted that this relationship between trot and canter is not only important for pupils who are serious about their flatwork, but also for those whose main intention is to learn enough to hack in safety. It is not sufficient to teach such pupils a vague approximation of rising trot and hope that they can 'hang on' at canter. A rider of such little skill is highly unlikely to be able to control a horse at canter in the open, and will not only be in danger personally, but may endanger others close by.)

Another reason sometimes given for teaching rising trot first is that it protects horses from having beginners 'bumping about on their backs'. While it is true that carrying an unskilled novice at trot may be uncomfortable for a horse, I would contend that such discomfort will be *greater* if an unbalanced rider is rising badly, pulling him or herself out of the saddle via the reins, and thumping back down onto the cantle.

If, then, an instructor is to spend time in helping pupils to achieve sitting trot, he or she should outline the reasons for doing so and explain that, while it may take a little time to 'get the hang of it', this will be time well spent. It may be possible to draw useful analogies with other activities where certain foundations must be laid before progress can be made, for example, a golfer will never play to a reasonable standard without a passably good grip, and a musician will not get far if he or she tries to avoid pieces containing initially difficult chords – instead, the novice musician must learn to master them, thereby improving both repertoire and dexterity.

It will be helpful in the early stages of teaching sitting trot if leaders are still available – failing which, the instructor may have to assume this role. The main function of the leaders is to ensure that the trot is rhythmic and reasonably active, but the fact that they are effectively controlling the horses lessens the need for riders to take a significant contact, and consequently lessens any tendency to use the reins for security.

Having checked that the pupils' posture is correct at walk, they can be told to hold lightly under the front saddle arch with the inside hand to help maintain the seat, and asked to trot on for a few strides, making a conscious effort not to clench their buttocks or draw up their legs. It is much better to accustom pupils to the movement of trot a few strides at a time, than to push them to a point where they feel uncomfortable or insecure. Similarly, it is better not to ask them to trot without stirrups at too early a stage. Indeed, early efforts at trot may give practical guidance as to whether stirrup leathers are at a suitable length; overshort leathers may make it more difficult for riders to maintain seat contact, and overlong leathers may result in irons being readily lost.

Once pupils are able to perform a passable sitting trot, they can be introduced to the rising version, and should find the transition relatively simple, as they will already be accustomed to the rhythm of the gait. If ensuing trot work involves frequent changes from one version to the other, this will help familiarise them with both, and will also be a useful exercise in posture control.

Understanding Initial Attitudes to Learning
Continuing the proposition that pupils should be treated as individuals, it is worth noting that different people will, for

different reasons, exhibit varied approaches and attitudes to learning. Therefore, if an instructor is to be fully effective, he or she must not only adapt to varying rates of technical progress but also tailor his or her approach and responses in the light of these attitudes.

Given that there are probably as many different approaches to learning as there are pupils, it is not possible to make an exhaustive study of what an instructor may have to contend with, but common generalities would include the following points.

Some pupils tend to stop concentrating on other issues when listening to or discussing a particular point. (This trait sometimes extends, in private lessons, to the pupil stopping riding altogether in order to enter into debate.) Although the recognition that such pupils are giving the instruction their attention can be reassuring, there can be disruptive connotations, ranging from a leading file taking the ride in the wrong direction to a pupil forgetting to attend to one issue of posture or aid application when concentrating upon another. With such pupils it is important to emphasise that the substance of a command or suggestion should be additional to, not a replacement for, other correct actions already being taken (for example, 'Keep the rein contact, but use your legs to ask the horse to move forwards more actively'). However, with such pupils, the instructor should, where practical, recognise their 'one thing at a time' approach, and aim for step-by-step improvement, rather than trying to bombard them with a series of different (albeit related) instructions.

Regarding the issue of concentration, there are some pupils who will habitually look at the instructor when addressed. While this is generally indicative of good manners and paying attention, it should be explained that it is not necessary in the context of a riding lesson, and may actually be undesirable. In extreme cases, it could result in a collision and otherwise tends to promote crookedness in the rider and, consequentially, the horse. Sometimes, however, the action may be associated with impaired hearing and, in such cases, the instructor must do all he or she can to ensure audibility.

Those pupils who are really keen will tend to do their own research from an early stage. This most commonly takes the form of reading, but may also include watching instructional videos, attending lectures or demonstrations, and so on. Such pupils are the most likely to ask questions, often triggered by actual or perceived connections between something the instructor says and something noted during their research. Where such interest is shown, it should be acknowledged by a full, correct answer, but the instructor should be prepared to tailor the timing of the response according to the immediate relevance of the enquiry. If it is specifically relevant to a certain instruction or exercise, it should be dealt with at the earliest opportunity. If, however, it is of general interest but not immediately relevant, it can be addressed during a break or at the end of the lesson, as previously mentioned. What an instructor must not do in the case of a genuine enquiry is dismiss it with a response along the lines of 'You don't need to worry about that until you're more advanced'. This, to my mind, is intensely patronising, and likely to dampen enthusiasm. It may also give a perceptive pupil cause to wonder whether it is a smokescreen for the instructor's own ignorance or uncertainty.

One complication of pupils doing their own research is that it can lead to minor obsessions with misunderstood or partially understood concepts. These are often manifest by some exaggerated mannerism of posture or aid application, which must be remedied before becoming an ingrained bad habit. It should be stressed that, in order to do this effectively, it is necessary to gain a full insight into the misconception and explain why it is such; it is no good simply saying 'Don't do that' to a pupil who is thinking (albeit wrongly) 'But Reiner Klimke (or whoever) says I should'.

Another issue arising from pupils' research (or lack of it) is that, in extreme cases, an instructor may meet some pupils who want to discuss the theory of everything to the point of exhaustion, and others who have no interest in theory and believe they will learn only by doing. In each case (and especially if both types are present in the same class!) it is important for the instructor to strike a balance. On the one hand, he or she must convince the theoreticians that, without being translated into practice, theory is mere abstraction, while on the other hand, he or she must convince the rabid practitioners that, unless they understand what they are trying to achieve and how to do it, they will have little chance of success.

One corollary to striking the balance between theory and practice is that it may occasionally be expedient for the instructor to get on a horse and demonstrate a point. At such times, it is important to remember that the object of the exercise is not to show off, but to show *how*. Further to this, while it is possible that the instructor will be trying to assist a pupil with a particular problem, there should be no hint of 'You can't ride that horse – let me get on and do it properly', but rather 'Let me feel what the problem is, show you why you are having trouble, and show you how you can overcome it.' To this end, if the pupil has a particular riding fault that is causing or exacerbating the problem, the instructor should be prepared to demonstrate this to show that the horse will go incorrectly specifically because of that fault, rather than because of who is riding. If the instructor then rides without exhibiting this fault, and the horse goes better, he or she will have given a valuable and graphic demonstration. If, however, the instructor simply gets on and rides the horse well, little will have been demonstrated beyond the fact that the instructor rides better than the pupil, which, presumably, is only to be expected.

Leading on from this, it is especially important that an instructor acknowledges different individuals' attitudes to criticism. One may, for example, come upon hearty, robust characters who say things such as, 'I'm here to learn. If I'm riding like a raving idiot, don't be afraid to say so.' While such attitudes are usually genuine, it would be undiplomatic – if not unprofessional – to take the offer too literally and, given that an instructor should appear even-handed to all pupils, it would obviously be inappropriate to deal with all clients in such a manner. Indeed, the opposite attitude will be apparent in those who always react defensively to criticism by trying to find a justification for their actions. With such pupils it is essential to be very logical and explicit, both so that they are less likely to sense any element of personal criticism, and also so they are less able to engineer a defence that is plausible to themselves. With all pupils, of course, criticism should be comprehensible and constructive, and it will be better received and more effective if it is balanced by ready praise whenever praise is due.

Lastly, it should be noted that, in general, mature pupils do not enjoy being 'quizzed', especially on an individual basis. By quizzed, I do not mean asked for legitimate information, as when enquiring of a new pupil 'Have you done any work at canter yet?' or even asking a genuine 'Do you understand?' I am referring, rather to the type of question designed to check up on the recipient, along the lines of 'Have you been listening?' or 'Do you remember?'. While such questions may be well received by a youngster anxious to show off, a mature person will generally derive little satisfaction from answering correctly, and nothing but embarrassment from answering wrongly. Therefore, even if an instructor does believe that a pupil has forgotten something (or has not been listening), it is much more diplomatic and productive to ask 'Is *everyone* clear about the aids/exercise?' (offering a chance for anyone unsure to say so), than to ask 'Mr . . ., can you tell us the aids for . . .?', which rather begs the response 'No I can't, because your teaching has not made it sufficiently clear.'

CHAPTER NINE

Progression

Once pupils are established in the basics, the instructor's role is to assist those with specific ambitions to achieve them, and to persuade the less ambitious of the value of continual progress, both in the hope that this may fuel further ambition and in the interests of their greater enjoyment and safety. With regard to the latter, it cannot be overemphasised that there is no 'minimum level of competence' that will guarantee a rider's safety – indeed, an element of risk will always exist, although it will tend to decrease as a rider's skill increases. Therefore, when teaching pupils who 'just want to learn enough to hack out', an instructor should take pains to emphasise that the more accomplished they become, the more they will be able to do, in greater safety and on a greater variety of horses. What he or she should *not* do, however, is attempt to frighten pupils into seeking greater competence, or risk losing their attention by placing too much *abstract* emphasis on the finer points of equitation. Such pupils are likely to be more perceptive to learning movements such as turn on the forehand, leg-yielding and rein back in the context of gate-opening manoeuvres than as 'dressage', and may find more value in shoulder-in as a counter to potential shying than as an end in itself.

By emphasising the value of continual learning in the context of individual requirements, the instructor should be able to sustain each pupil's sense of purpose and create the best climate for a continued programme of cohesive and interesting lessons.

As we have seen, however, individual requirements are attended by individual aptitudes and attitudes and an instructor must be aware that this state of affairs is a continual, indeed developing, one. Further to this, while we have already examined some general attitudes to learning in the context of essential basics, consideration should now be given to attitudes toward what become, effectively and increasingly, options. To define this idea further, we might argue that if people are to ride at all, they must be prepared to learn certain basic aids. However, they do not necesarily *have* to learn to jump, ride walk to canter transitions, ride in traffic, and so on. Therefore, if an instructor is really concerned to educate, improve, and 'take the pupils with him', he will need to understand, and work with, their attitudes to such options.

One general difference between youngsters and adults is their attitude towards failure. Unless they have previous evidence to the contrary, youngsters tend to assume that things will go well, and may become resentful of agencies other than themselves if this does not happen. Adults, however, often anticipate the possibility of failure and, while they may be embarrassed by it, they are more likely to blame themselves than others. In simple equestrian terms, we might generalise that if a youngster cannot achieve a certain result on a horse, his of her primary tendency will be to blame the horse, whereas mature people in the same circumstances will tend primarily to blame themselves. If, then, a teacher of youngsters needs to persuade them of the possibility that a fault may lie at *their* door, conversely, a teacher of mature riders may have to persuade them that problems are not inevitably the result of their own errors and that, even when certain failings on their part contribute to a problem, the aim is to rectify this, rather than simply being self-deprecating or apologetic.

The instructor should, therefore, make it understood that pupils are *allowed* to fail, provided that they are trying, and are willing to learn from the failure. This should help to avoid two potential problem areas: first, where a pupil is expecting to make a mess of something and is embarrassed by the thought of doing so while appearing to try hard, and therefore makes a flippant, half-hearted effort before saying, 'I knew I'd get that wrong'; second, where a pupil is so determined to avoid the embarrassment of failure that he or she tries *too* hard (i.e. overrides), thereby creating a new problem.

Notwithstanding this attitude towards failure, it remains better, where appropriate, to *persuade* pupils to attempt 'optional' work, rather than trying to pressurise them into it. A good reason for this is that if a pupil needs to be pressurised, this signifies reluctance and negativity, which do not auger well for success, and failure in such circumstances may well be used to justify their initial reluctance and/ or be blamed upon the person who applied the pressure. In any event, the outcome is not likely to be constructive.

Similarly, an instructor should try to avoid putting peer pressure on pupils. This can occur if it is *assumed* that the whole class will wish to try something, in which case a pupil with reservations may feel awkward about appearing the odd one out. The chances of this happening will be lessened if the instructor works on the basis of allowing pupils to opt *in* ('Who wants to try . . .?') rather than opting out ('Is there anyone who doesn't want to . . .?'). It should be stressed that if someone opts out of a certain exercise, a relevant and useful alternative should be suggested: a pupil should not normally be given a choice between doing something he or shes does not wish to do, or doing nothing at all.

Further to this, an instructor should also be prepared to act with sensitivity on those occasions when he or she believes that a pupil should not perform a certain exercise. Sometimes, reasons can be given quite plainly, especially where they are obviously in the pupil's interest – for example, avoiding some action that might aggravate an injury. On other occasions, a degree of diplomacy may be called for, in which case the explanation of an alternative exercise can help enhance one's reasoning. For example, 'I don't think your horse is listening to the aids well enough to do a good walk to canter at present, so for now I'd like you to gain his attention by riding a series of walk-trot-halt transitions' is more tactful and useful than 'It's no good your trying this exercise; you can't get your horse on the aids'.

A situation that combines aspects of peer pressure with an instructor's judgement of what is appropriate may arise if ambitious pupils make requests to do things currently beyond their – or other class members' – abilities. With mature riders, such requests are rarely made out of bravado; the most likely cause is overenthusiasm. If, however, such requests are very frequent and from different sources, the instructor will have to consider whether they stem from boredom and frustration with his or her teaching!

For reasons of practicality and diplomacy, it is preferable, as far as possible, to pre-empt such requests; to some extent, this will be a natural product of good teaching practice, whereby pupils will understand the need for logical pro-gression and be aware of, and broadly satisfied with, the progress they are making. Furthermore, if overambitious requests are made within this context, it will be easier for an instructor to explain why they cannot be met at present, and how what *is* presently being done is paving the way towards them.

The somewhat 'elastic' approach to individual needs previously outlined may also help to pre-empt requests to do things that are beyond the scope of some class members, simply by avoiding all work being tailored to the standard of the less able. Another useful ploy – subject to constraints of safety and practicality – is the regular swapping of horses. This may, for example, prevent a pupil on a more talented horse from making overambitious requests based on a false perspective of his or her own ability, as well as giving the rider 'swapped' onto it a little encouragement.

Before leaving this topic, it should be stressed that what we are concerned with here are *overambitious* requests; that is to say requests to do things that, given the pupils' current ability, would be unacceptably risky or so unlikely to succeed that they would have no positive value. Pre-empting such requests is a very different matter from generally listening to requests or suggestions, which is a desirable part of communication between pupil and teacher. In general, the instructor should welcome such communication and, if he or she feels that something requested would be universally relevant and beneficial, the good instructor should be prepared to act upon it. In addition to generally 'satisfying the customers', such compliance will tend to *reinforce* the instructor's authority on those occasions where a request has to be denied.

An instructor of mature pupils should, then, take account of their approach to learning and remain considerate of any relevant infirmities. Apart from any individual adjustment necessitated by the latter, however, there is no reason why the purely technical side of their instruction should depart from established principles of equitation. Since these are widely acknowledged, and expounded in many other books, it is not my intention to reiterate them in any detail. However, a few major topics are worth considering briefly in the context of mature riders.

The Underlying Principle

If we accept that we are, in the main, dealing with intelligent people who genuinely want to learn, then we must be certain to promote a basis that makes this possible. The underlying principle of correct riding is that a horse must be ridden 'from the back to the front'; the rider producing forward movement with seat and legs, and receiving it/metering it out with his or her hands. A rider must, therefore, understand that the correct execution of any movement is dependent upon establishing in the horse a desire to move forwards, and then directing that movement as required by correct use of the appropriate aids.

The main reason for riding in this manner is that the horse is thus encouraged to move forwards and enabled to do so correctly and in balance, thereby making its own task more pleasant and the rider's easier. The converse of this – bad movement caused by bad riding – causes or provokes many problems and evasions in the horse that make the rider's task difficult and uncomfortable; indeed, it produces horses patently unsuitable for mature riders, especially those in less than perfect physical condition.

A teacher of mature riders should, therefore, be especially vigilant in promoting this principle, and his or her teaching should emphasise that, far from being a theoretical ideal, it is of fundamental practical importance. If the instructor is to achieve this, it will be apparent that he or she cannot pay lip service to the idea and then give commands that contradict it, so care must be taken to use appropriate terminology – '*Open* the left rein' not 'Pull on the left rein'; 'Ride *forward* into halt' not 'Come back to halt'; 'Ease down' not 'Pull up', and so on.

Canter Work

As previously mentioned, insufficient preparation before introducing canter is often the cause of first falls. Therefore, whatever route an instructor takes the pupils through the basics, it is essential that they are able to perform passable sitting trot before being asked to canter. As, in early attempts at canter, it is quite possible that pupils will draw their legs up and lose their stirrups, it is helpful if they have had some prior experience of riding without stirrups, in order that any such loss does not lead to panic or loss of balance. Such experience is likely to have been gained as an element of learning sitting trot, and is another reason for its importance.

Pupils with weaker seats – whether due to infirmities or not – should be introduced to canter on horses with relatively long strides and smooth gaits, although length of stride should not be allied to a tendency to move too fast in canter. All pupils, in fact, should begin canter on well-balanced, amenable horses; any that canter significantly on the forehand, regardless of temperament, are unsuitable, as they can convey an (admittedly false) impression that they are pulling or trying to run away. It is also good policy to reintroduce neckstraps prior to the first canter, although it should be stressed that this is not because the gait is inherently dangerous or difficult, but simply because it is new and different.

When explaining the aids to canter, it is important to emphasise that a horse does not need to go faster before it can canter, but it will go somewhat faster *as a result* of cantering.

It may, in fact, be helpful if the instructor demonstrates this by riding a few walk to canter transitions. Furthermore, a close view of a horse covering the ground at a steady, rhythmical canter may help dispel any preconceptions of 'wall of death' laps of the arena from pupils' minds. This, in turn, makes it more likely that they will 'allow' their horses into the gait, rather than setting their hands against an imagined 'taking off'.

When explaining the canter aids, it is inevitable that the subject of the leading leg will arise. While this is fundamentally important, I do not believe that an instructor should make a meal of it too soon; doing so can cause pupils to become obsessed with the correct lead to the extent that they form the habit of leaning forward to look for it when giving the aids, thereby reducing the effectiveness of the seat and inducing crookedness. Instead, while explaining the need for the correct lead in terms of balance, and the consequent need for precise aids, instructors should allow pupils to get on with obtaining canter and check the lead themselves. Should it be wrong, a pupil must, of course, be told to return to trot, but quietly, not by shouting 'Wrong leg, wrong leg'. This, in turn, emphasises the point that when being taught canter, pupils must be taught the *downward* transition as well as the upward one: if a horse is already unbalanced by being on the wrong lead, it is hardly desirable to have the rider trying to pull it back into trot via the reins.

It may help both in obtaining the correct lead and in preventing pupils from making their horses 'run' in trot if

'I know it's down there somewhere!' Leaning forward to look for the leading leg

upward transitions to canter are sometimes made after crossing a long diagonal – for example, a transition to right canter might be ridden after crossing the FH diagonal, just after regaining the outside track at H.

Jumping
Jumping is perhaps the prime example of 'optional' riding. An instructor providing jumping tuition for novice pupils would be well advised to keep the points made above at the

forefront of his or her thoughts, remembering in particular that negative, uncommitted riding is the root cause of many jumping problems.

It should also be borne in mind that many inexperienced riders will have somewhat distorted preconceptions about jumping. Some may, for example, equate jumping primarily with their experience of watching major competitions on television, and have the notion that it is necessarily a very formidable undertaking. Others, with either a broader overview or a more intrepid outlook, may pick up on perceptions of glamour, excitement and challenge. Either way, the prospect of jumping tends to heighten the emotions, inducing some degree of trepidation or excitement. It is a fundamental task for the instructor to neutralise such emotions to the extent that jumping is approached with due care, but without fear; with due commitment, but without recklessness. The best basis for this is to ensure that jumping is not portrayed as a separate endeavour, but simply as another aspect of riding, where the horse is asked to perform a task of which it is naturally capable, and where the basic principles of equitation continue to apply.

To be consistent with this philosophy, the instructor should, in practice, teach jumping on a regular, progressive basis, the aim being to produce pupils who can *ride* safely and effectively over a straightforward course of jumps, as opposed to being able to stay on somehow over an isolated miniscule obstacle. It will be apparent, therefore, that the ocasional 'pop' over crossed poles in the final minutes of a lesson does not constitute effective jumping instruction; indeed it will merely frustrate the keener pupils, while failing to persuade the less committed that jumping is worthwhile.

If it is important that pupils progress correctly to riding at canter, it is even more so that they progress correctly to riding over jumps. It is not feasible to teach jumping, in any meaningful sense, to a pupil who cannot ride with reasonable control and security at walk, trot and canter, and starting jumping too soon is a recipe for disaster. At best, it will confuse, discourage, frustrate and create bad habits; at worst, it will cause unnecessary falls and, perhaps, injury. It is, therefore, essential that an instructor does not allow himself to be pressurised into starting jumping tuition by overeager, underexperienced pupils. Faced with this, the most constructive course is to explain that successful jumping is largely based on the ability to apply the principles of riding on the flat in a manner that permits the accurate presentation of the horse at its fences. This should diminish any concept of jumping as a separate issue and provide the pupils with an added incentive to improve their flatwork.

An instructor (or anybody else responsible for placing pupils) should also be wary of placing a new pupil straight into a lesson involving jumping. It is much preferable for such pupils to be assessed first on the flat, and this can be done either by automatically placing new pupils in flat lessons or, if jumping instruction has been specifically requested, arranging a private assessment before the new client joins a class.

As jumping makes greater demands on the athleticism of horse and rider than flatwork, and also places greater stresses on tack, the instructor must give increased attention to these matters. Because of the postural adaptation and increased mobility required of the rider, it does not necessarily follow that a pupil who is just fit enough to cope with flatwork will manage as well over jumps. In some cases, therefore, it may be necessary to tailor a pupil's ambitions in this field: however much he or she wishes to help the pupils, an instructor who truly has their interests at heart will not encourage them to do anything that, given their circumstances, entails an unacceptable degree of risk.

A common-sense acknowledgement of the heightened impact of general 'wear and tear' is also called for. An instructor should not, for example, expect mature pupils with stiff backs or weak legs to ride *ad nauseam* around the arena in posed 'jumping position'. This sort of exercise is, in fact, pretty worthless for anyone, but if it renders pupils too stiff and tired to ride effectively when they actually start to jump, it becomes counter-productive.

While it is desirable for pupils to start jumping on those horses with which they are familiar, the most important criteria are the attitude and aptitude of the horse. Furthermore, the benefits of jumping familiar horses will be reduced if their usual tack is not appropriate for the purpose. Therefore, in addition to giving attention to the condition of tack, it should also be assessed as to its suitability for jumping. Specifically, saddles should be of jumping or general purpose type (not dressage or showing), stirrup leathers should be capable of adjustment to the user's jumping length and reins should be neither too short nor unduly long. For early lessons, and until pupils are secure and technically competent, neckstraps should be fitted as standard.

Riding Out
Riding out is something that most pupils look forward to, indeed it is the main reason for many people taking lessons in the first place. Furthermore, confident and capable riding in the open is a fundamental prerequisite for many eques-

96

trian sports. This being so, it is an important part of an instructor's role to ensure that pupils become competent in this area, either in order that they can derive maximum enjoyment from hacking, or as a foundation for participating in their chosen discipline. Obviously, the groundwork for this is incorporated in work done in the arena, but the teaching process can and should continue when pupils are out in the open. In this respect, there are a number of points to be borne in mind.

First, it should be explained that when horses go out in groups they will, in effect, be in their natural herd environment, and their natural instincts will thus be heightened. This will apply, to some extent, to all horses, including those basically well schooled and well mannered. It is likely, therefore, that all horses will be a little keener outside than when in the school, and they may tend to mimic each others' actions, shy at movements in the undergrowth and try to snatch the odd mouthful of foliage. While an instructor should not make a major issue of such matters, advance warning will prevent pupils from thinking that this behaviour is exceptional, and practical advice will help them to deal with it effectively. For example, explaining in advance that a horse may attempt to eat, and how to dissuade it from doing so, may prevent a rider from straining his or her back in trying to pull the horse's head up with the reins, or even save a horse from poisoning. In general terms, pupils should be advised that it may be necessary to apply the aids more firmly than usual on any occasion when their horses' attention is, or is likely to be, distracted by any outside agency – though it should be stressed that 'more firmly' does not imply 'roughly' or 'improperly'. It should also be mentioned that while riders are quite entitled to enjoy the countryside, they must never assume that their horses are on 'automatic pilot'; indeed, they have a responsibility to themselves and others to remain attentive and in control.

Such issues assume even greater importance if, as is increasingly likely, going out entails some riding on public roads. Here it should be emphasised that, while escorts will take every possible measure to ensure safety, only the rider has ultimate control of his or her horse. (This does not mean that a rider is necessarily to blame for any misfortune, but he or she is certainly the final agent for its avoidance.) For novice riders under escort, the main concerns are that they do not allow their horses to run up the backside of another, nor to dawdle and risk other road users splitting the ride. It is also important that pupils understand how to recognise and pass any object that could potentially frighten a horse. In this respect, they must first be taught that horses do not always perceive things in the same way as people, and that objects must therefore be evaluated from the *horse's* point of view. In the presence of anything suspect, a rider must *not* tense up (especially in the hands), but ride firmly forwards, taking as wide a route as is safely practical round the obstacle with the horse's head turned a little away from it, and apply the 'outside' leg firmly on the horse's side. Those riders who have learnt the rudiments of shoulder-in will be familiar with these principles and will be more likely to avoid the heat-of-the-moment error of trying to hold the horse straight by pulling on the rein nearer the suspicious object.

The other major issue is what is actually *done* when riding out. If there is to be educational value in such ventures, it follows that a progressive programme should be applied. On the first couple of occasions that pupils ride out, the main concern should be to familiarise them with the

Not to dawdle and risk other road users splitting the ride

aforementioned principles of riding in a new environment, and this should take place in the context of fairly sedate hacking. Gradually, however, an instructor can introduce two aspects of riding that cannot be properly addressed in the teaching arena: riding up and down hills, and exercising control at the faster gaits.

The extent to which the former can be achieved will depend largely on the local terrain, although much useful

99

work can be done on relatively minor banks and hillocks. This is helpful both as an introduction for those who may progress to various forms of cross-country riding and in improving the balance and 'feel' for movement of all riders.

The issue of control at speed is a major one, to which too little attention is given. Riding at the faster gaits in the open should be taught with the same thoroughness as school movements; indeed, it can be argued that the ability to control a fast-moving horse may be of more practical value than the ability to look polished in the arena. To this end, the instructor should explain the role of shortened stirrup leathers in providing a basis for a posture that allows the horse to move with maximum ease in the faster gaits, but which can be readily adapted, if necessary, to apply driving aids or to exercise effective restraint. Since this posture has much in common with jumping postures, the principles will be readily absorbed by pupils who have received jumping instruction. It can and should, however, be understood and employed by all who wish to ride at the faster gaits, as it will greatly assist a rider to travel at the speed he or she wishes, rather than that solely dictated by the horse.

In addition to the purely technical aspects of control, an instructor can help pupils by stressing the importance of riding transitions to canter in a correct, controlled fashion, and establishing the gait at a steady rhythm before asking the horse to quicken as required. In any circumstance where pupils are to canter one at a time, those waiting for their turn should be dissuaded from making the instinctive error of turning their horses to face away from their departing fellows; this upsets many horses, and may result in them whipping round and getting 'first run' on their riders, or even unshipping them.

Other common-sense measures that can be taken to assist pupils include paying attention to the positioning of individual horses in the ride, and cantering only where there is a safe and well-defined stopping area at the end of the proposed route. Classically, of course, the instructor (and all relevant staff at a riding establishment) should not allow horses to get into the habit of anticipating cantering or galloping in certain places; even if suitable locations are limited, their use should still be rotated and, ideally, horses should walk or trot in such places more often than they canter.

Falls

Although an instructor should do everything within his or her powers to ensure the safety of the pupils, it would be unrealistic to assume that none of them will ever have a fall. This being so, the instructor must always be prepared to deal with the situation sympathetically, and take appropriate action in the event of injury.

In the unfortunate event of a pupil sustaining serious injury, it is of paramount importance that no unqualified person attempts assistance beyond their competence, and that professional help is summoned as quickly as possible. It can greatly assist medical personnel if they are advised of any pre-existing condition or infirmity of the victim. In some cases, this may still be pertinent even if it does not seem directly related to their apparent injuries. This is another reason to ascertain the existence of any such conditions, beyond their relevance to everyday instruction.

In a number of cases, pupils may sustain what can be broadly described as minor injuries; that is to say, they do not appear to require immediate professional assistance, but are not entirely unscathed. Assessing the effect of such injuries is largely a matter of applying common sense to individual cases, but certain principles should be borne in mind.

First, an instructor should not allow or encourage a pupil to remount without first enquiring as to his or her well-being. Even if the pupil claims to be fit to continue, the instructor should not permit this if he or she has serious doubts about the advisability of their doing so. Dubious claims to being 'all right' can derive from an adult being anxious not to make a fuss, or from hardened sportsmen who are used to taking a knock, but who may not have the experience to evaluate the effect of an injury on their ability to ride. While an instructor may commend such robust attitudes in principle, he or she should be prepared to override them in practice if they seem contrary to the pupil's welfare.

It is also possible that pupils may wish to remount as a result of having been told that they must do so immediately after a fall if they are not to lose their nerve. While it is good practice for an *uninjured* rider to remount promptly (there being no reason not to), this rather silly myth is a very poor reason for an *unfit* rider to do so – the injured condition merely increasing the likelihood of a further fall which may result in serious injury and actual loss of confidence. Any pupils who have been misled in this way should, therefore, be disabused of this notion, and reassured that they will be given every chance and assistance to regain any lost confidence once their physical condition allows.

In any case, where the pupil is dubious about his or her own condition, the instructor should err on the side of caution and prescribe a period of rest, and should certainly never badger a pupil into remounting, regardless of what the pupil's own assessment of his or her condition may be. One type of fall that might be included in this category is that which, without causing serious injury, produces a shock reaction. This can be particularly unpleasant for a mature person who has no wish to make a fuss but is unable to control the reaction and is embarrassed by it as well as suffering from the physical effects of the fall. Once it has been established that no serious injury or concussion has occurred (which should be done with care as shock can be associated with major injury), the most positive response is to acknowledge the presence of shock, and then assist the victim to a warm comfortable place where he or she may sit quietly. Do not provide a hot drink unless you are sure the person is quite uninjured. Once the initial trauma is past in such circumstances, adults usually prefer to be left alone, although a responsible person should enquire as to their well-being after a short interval. If a pupil suffers a fall of this type, the door should always be left open for a return to the saddle once he or she feels capable, even if this means making an arrangement outside the framework of the lesson. This is not because this person will necessarily suffer an actual 'loss of nerve' if they do not do so, but because the recent trauma may have created anxiety about the possibility of this; a situation that is best resolved positively at the earliest opportunity.

In those cases where no injury is sustained, the instructor can simply assist the pupil back into the saddle and continue the business of instruction, but he or she should also consider whether this ought to include an analysis of *why* the fall occurred. Although an instructor should never scold or belittle a pupil who has just suffered the indignity of a fall, it is a fact that the majority of falls by novice riders are rooted in some technical error or lack of foresight on their part. (It is certainly to be hoped that they do not arise from bad instruction, failure of tack or blatantly unsuitable horses.) If it is part of an instructor's job to correct relatively minor errors in pupils, it will be apparent that there is also a duty to draw a pupil's attention (tactfully) to any error great enough to part him or her from the mount. Although this will certainly not be a primary consideration in the case of an injured rider, logical extension suggests that if injury was the ultimate result of an error, this, too, should be addressed in an appropriate manner at an appropriate time.

Whenever a fall has occurred, the appropriate details should be entered in the stables' or instructor's own 'accident book'. This information should give an exact description of what happened and name any witnesses who were present. This should be done following any accident involving any client, but is especially important with mature clients who may have sustained more severe injuries than at first appears to be the case.

CHAPTER TEN

Further Education

We have already noted that many keen pupils will seek sources of education additional to their lessons, and that this is likely to be an ongoing, expanding process. Furthermore, while not everyone will be sufficiently committed to fill their bookshelves with equestrian literature, it is likely that appropriate stimuli from beyond the framework of lessons will enhance the interest of all pupils. An astute instructor will recognise these facts and understand the consequential benefits of giving appropriate advice, guidance and encouragement. By acting to increase the knowledge and enthusiasm of the pupils, the instructor will not only help them but will, in turn, make his or her own task easier and more fulfilling. The vehicles for this are, perhaps, more numerous than one might initially expect. They include:

Lectures/Demonstrations
Recommending good speakers who will address interesting topics has much in common with recommending good books, but may have the added glamour of a 'live' performance by an eminent rider. Recommendations should, however, be made with some care as, while some topics or personalities have almost universal appeal, others are of a more 'specialised interest'.

Spectating
The prospect of spectating at major events is likely to have wide appeal but where an instructor is able to attend with pupils, he or she has the opportunity to motivate them beyond simply marvelling at mighty feats of equitation to *learning* from them. Simple examples would include pointing out:

> The way horse-trial riders seek to settle their mounts into a rhythm, and the varied approaches and postures they adopt when tackling different obstacles.
>
> The difference between impulsion and speed as highlighted by the way showjumpers tackle large fences.
>
> The evidence from the dressage arena that equine energy is to be *harnessed*, not wasted or destroyed.
>
> The way in which race riders control their mounts at speed.

There is also value in pupils spectating at local shows, as they will be more readily able to identify with the participants and this will, perhaps, broaden their perspective and encourage them to think about having a go themselves. This is also a factor in:

Learning Through Assisting
Activities such as stewarding, jump-judging, scoring and writing for dressage judges will all help people to improve their knowledge of what is involved in the various disciplines. This is particularly useful for those with competitive ambitions, and also for fostering such ambitions.

Introduction to Riding Clubs
This may be closely connected with helping at local shows.

A 'textbook' posture (*above*) and something less so (*below*).
Learning by watching others

Those clubs with a policy of encouraging novices – especially those that cater for non-owners – can provide a solid base for progression. In addition to organising lectures, trips and so on, they can introduce members to the system of grade tests (the stable management sections of which are especially instructive for prospective owners/sharers), and also to the increasingly relevant Riding and Road Safety test. All pupils who ride on the roads should be encouraged to take this, and it is worth stressing that it is not, primarily, a test of riding skill, but a means of educating riders in the relevant sections of the Highway Code and in safe practice in potentially risky situations.

CHAPTER ELEVEN

Advising on the Purchase of a Horse

One consequence of instructing is the possibility of being asked for advice by a pupil who is considering purchasing a horse. The first point to bear in mind is that being asked for such advice does not simply afford an opportunity to show off one's knowledge of conformation; rather, it imposes a responsibility that needs handling with due care and caution in the interests of pupil, horse and the instructor's reputation.

If, in the instructor's opinion, the pupil concerned is insufficiently experienced to enjoy and benefit from horse ownership, he or she should try – diplomatically but determinedly – to persuade the pupil to wait for a while. Reasons that can be cited are:

1) If the pupil exercises patience, he or she will be able to obtain greater benefit when he or she *does* make a purchase; the additional experience will enable the pupil to achieve quicker rapport with a new horse, and he or she will be capable of doing more with it.

2) Additional experience and skill will also permit a greater choice of purchase.

3) It should be emphasised that *whenever* a horse is ridden, its training is either advanced or retarded to some extent, and there is a considerable difference between riding under instruction and riding/schooling/managing a horse in isolation. (People who claim that they will only

ride under instruction inevitably, for a variety of reasons, fail to stick to this and it is, in any case, an unsustainably strict regime for an owner who rides basically for pleasure.)

This last point, although perhaps the most significant, is the one that needs putting with most tact, and it is also the one most likely to be conceded only in hindsight. It encapsulates the basic reason why, despite acquiring horses that are as suitable as circumstances permit, so many people condemn themselves and their horses to frustration and misery – that is, without supervision, there is no such animal as a total novice's ride.

With luck, a combination of these points will be accepted by a mature novice – the chances are at least better than in the case of an impatient youngster who is making life a misery for non-horsey parents.

Assuming that a pupil *is* considered a sufficiently experienced rider for horse ownership to be realistic, there is still much to consider before any viewing arrangements are made. In the first place, it is pointless obtaining a horse without having found accommodation that is suitable for both horse and owner. With regard to this, it should be borne in mind that good yards often have waiting lists and, if accommodation is found in a panic, its suitability may simply be a matter of luck. In the second place, it is pointless finding suitable accommodation and then being unable to pay for it on a regular basis. These two issues lie hand in glove at the very foundations of horse ownership, and must be fully resolved before any further steps are taken.

Although it might seem logical to resolve the question of cost *before* viewing accommodation, this matter is not necessarily as clear-cut as it might appear. The main reason

Without supervision there is no such thing as a novice ride

for this lies in the risk that enthusiastic would-be owners may readily be tempted into an arrangement that suits their pocket but, in other respects, suits neither themselves nor their horse. Such people are more likely to be dissuaded from taking rash steps if they first gain some knowledge of the alternative facilities available, and can thus form a broader view of what they really want from ownership.

Even where such risks are not apparent, there is much to be said for the concept of 'shopping around' for the most suitable accommodation, and then making a decision based not just on actual cost, but on value for money. While suitable accommodation and its cost can never be

111

considered as entirely separate issues, I would suggest that anyone advising a new owner should place primary emphasis on suitability, and that is the first matter we shall consider.

Where first-time owners are concerned, do-it-yourself and part livery are usually best avoided. The former can be fraught with all sorts of difficulties, and may prove unimaginably stressful and time-consuming for a new-comer. Furthermore, the 'experienced friend who can help' with such arrangements will inevitably be ill/on holiday/at a show when most needed, and may quickly find that constant demands upon their expertise become irritatingly disruptive of their own regime. In fact, for a new owner with work and family commitments, do-it-yourself is probably only worth even *considering* if they have stabling facilities at home.

Part livery is something of a catch-all term, but often involves an arrangement whereby the yard performs basic duties for a reduced fee, and charges on an individual basis for other tasks carried out at the owners' request on occasions when the owners cannot do these themselves. The drawback with this is that if an owner has less free time than he or she anticipated, or is otherwise a victim of circumstances, he or she may end up paying more than under a full livery agreement, with the added complication that stable staff may not know from day to day what is expected of them.

Bearing these points in mind, it is generally preferable if new owners can keep their horses at full livery at a reputable yard. Although such yards are less common than one would hope, an instructor with local knowledge may be able to suggest somewhere suitable. Of course, in doing so the instructor must take account of various factors that are pertinent to the individual concerned. These should include:

Accessibility
It is probable that most mature riders will have their own transport. If this is the case, it will not be essential for the stable to be on their doorstep. Although no one will wish to spend too much time travelling, a moderate journey to an eminently suitable yard may be well worthwhile.

For mature riders, suitability of location may not be dictated solely by where they live. Depending upon their regime, it may be more convenient if the stable is readily accessible from their workplace, although, ideally, it would be located somewhere convenient for both work and home.

Further to this, accessibility should be assessed not just in terms of travelling distance and time, but also the available riding time. This is important because the amount of time an owner can spend with the horse has a direct influence on the 'value' gained from ownership. In most cases, there will effectively be restrictions of some sort on a person's riding time, over and above the potential time they have available. These restrictions may consist of factors such as length of daytime in winter, possble lack of arena lighting, periods of heavy use of the arena, a yard's feeding arrangements, locking-up times, and so on. These must be evaluated in the context of other demands on an owner's time – for instance, circumstances that might be hopeless for nine-to-five worker may be very suitable for somebody on shiftwork, and vice versa, while an owner on flexitime might be able to work within all sorts of strange scenarios.

Exercise and Feeding Arrangements
A question that arises immediately out of the issue of riding

time is what will happen to the horse when the owner is not riding. If the owner is able to ride most days, provided the horse is being suitably fed, there is really no problem. If, however, the owner can ride only occasionally, or in sporadic spurts, it will be preferable if alternative exercising arrangements can be made. This begs the questions of whether exercising is included in the standard livery fee, how much it will otherwise cost, and what it consists of. What it *should* consist of is a regular, moderate amount of hacking out or basic schooling by a competent member of staff: clandestine use in a riding school, or the odd ten minutes' 'lungeing' by a slack-jawed incompetent come under the heading of 'rip-off'.

The question of feeding assumes great significance if the horse can only be ridden spasmodically. What will be required of the livery yard is a common-sense, individual approach, and this must be matched by the owner's realistic tailoring of his or her riding ambitions according to the horse's fitness. As far as the yard's approach is concerned, it has to be said that the old concept 'feed according to work done' appears generally to be on the decline. There are now too many places that rely on (dubious) theory rather than practical experience, and there can also be a tendency for yards where one type of horse predominates for *all* inmates to be fed on similar lines. Therefore, unless one is fully satisfied with a certain yard's feeding philosophy, it makes sense to recommend that a new owner chooses a yard where most of the horses are doing the same type of work he or she intends to do. This should circumvent the possibility of an occasional hacker having to contend with a horse fit for a day's hunting, or a cross-country enthusiast discovering that his or her horse is being fattened up for the show ring.

114

Facilities

There are two other advantages in choosing a yard that caters for like-minded riders. First, owners can enjoy the companionship and encouragement of people who share their interests (and perhaps share boxes to shows); second, such a yard is likely to offer appropriate facilities. The facilities on offer are an important consideration when assessing suitability and, again, they must be viewed in the light of an individual's requirements. If, for example, an owner is primarily interested in hacking, then ready access to pleasant, safe (well-drained!) countryside is fundamentally important. Use of an indoor arena might prove handy for the occasional lesson, or exercising in prolonged bad weather, but the availability of an immaculate cross-country course might arouse no interest at all. On the other hand, for an owner interested in competition, the arena and fences might be prerequisites; interest in the surrounding countryside being mainly confined to its adequacy for exercising.

Once suitable accommodation has been found, the question of finance can be addressed in more detail and on a more definite basis. At this point, it is essential to ensure that the potential owner is aware of, and has made provision for, supplementary financial factors such as insurance, uninsured vet's bills, shoeing, worming (if not included in the basic livery charge), boxing and upkeep or renewal of tack and clothing. With all such matters taken into account, a potential owner is finally in a position to judge whether he or she can – or wishes to – afford the upkeep of a horse. Should the decision be no, while this may cause initial disappointment, the efforts of the adviser will still have proved worthwhile: although there are many people who enjoy owning horses they can only *just* afford, it is unsatisfactory all round for somebody to own a horse he or she *just cannot* afford.

Sharing
Further to this, if a rider is seriously keen, but has decided that he or she cannot afford full ownership, it may be helpful to suggest seeking a 'share'. An increasing number of existing owners are becoming subject to the same pressures of time or money that may dissuade prospective owners from proceeding with purchase. However, in many cases, having already become owners, such people are understandably reluctant to relinquish their horses and therefore seek suitable people to share riding time and expenses. With due caution, common sense and a little luck, it is quite possible for a keen, competent rider to find a very worthwhile arrangement.

Briefly, the *advantages* of sharing are:

There is no capital outlay for purchase.

Weekly costs are usually no more than half the total cost of upkeep, and may be less; a sharer is not normally expected to contribute to the purchase of major items of tack or equipment, or to insurance premiums.

If sharing the right horse with the right owner, a sharer may gain a great deal of useful experience.

Although care is required in choosing a suitable 'share', this is no more than the care that would be required in purchasing a horse, and, if the arrangement does prove unsuitable, it is at least relatively easily terminated.

The potential *disadvantages* of sharing are:

The sharer does not have absolute control over what is done with the horse (although, for a less experienced person, this may be an advantage).

116

The sharer is not the sole – or necessarily major – beneficiary of the work he or she puts in, although, in a good arrangement, he or she should still feel very much 'part of the team'.

The major potential drawback for mature riders who work is that horse owners often work too, in which

Sharing: 'It was much more fun when you were behind'!

case they will naturally seek sharers whose riding time is complementary to their own. Thus, sharing is considerably less easy for those whose riding time is mainly restricted to weekends. However, those who have some flexibility of time may find this a real bonus, and it may help to open the door to a major opportunity.

Cost of Purchase

For those who decide they can afford to own a horse, the next question is how much they are prepared to pay for one. There will, of course, be the aspects of suitability to consider in conjunction with cost, but the first point to bear in mind is that a mature person, sufficiently solvent to keep a horse, should have little difficulty in raising a reasonable sum for purchase. It is, therefore, pretty unrealistic for a first-time owner to set a purchase figure that represents the rock-bottom of the market. Although real 'bargain buys' certainly exist, they are few and far between, and often prove bargains only because they go to an owner with specialist interests and/or well-developed skills. Thus, while a horse should not be rejected solely because it is cheap, it should certainly never be bought solely on that basis, and, for the average first-time owner, 'bargain hunting' is likely to prove a false economy. From an adviser's point of view, it is also likely to mean a lot of time wasted looking at 'duds', and may also indicate that the would-be owner is less sure of the available finances than he or she admits.

In many cases, however, the problem is not to persuade a purchaser to spend enough money, but to dissuade them from spending too much. This scenario is not uncommon with mature first-time buyers with significant finances but, although it may indicate an uninformed view of equine prices and values, the underlying reasons may be more complex than simply 'having more money than sense'. For example, a person whose general philosophy is 'you get what you pay for' may not just be in the habit of simply paying for luxury; they may also realise that, if one can afford it, top quality (usually expensive) goods and equipment may ultimately represent the best value. However, while this idea may hold good for a number of commodities, it can be less reliable in the equine world. This is because, first, most horses are a much more complex mixture of good points and drawbacks than the average new model car and, second, the capacity for equine excellence is at least as much in the hands of the rider as it is inherent in the horse. It is for this second reason, in particular, that relatively inexperienced riders with competitive ambitions should be discouraged from spending a lot of money on horses with 'great potential' (whether real or imagined). Such an arrangement is very different from buying a genuine 'schoolmaster', and the most likely consequence is not that the horse's potential will be fulfilled, but that the rider's inexperience will impair it and, in financial terms, devalue an expensive purchase.

Another circumstance in which a purchaser might be prepared to pay too much is when the prospect arises of buying a horse from a friend. Ironically, the potential drawbacks with such an arrangement can be rooted in the friendship itself; the potential purchaser will feel more at ease, may assume that the horse is in good physical condition and otherwise 'as stated', and will be less receptive to any suggestion that it may be overpriced, and therefore less inclined to negotiate. In saying this, I am not suggesting that everyone trying to sell a horse to a friend is out to cheat them, but simply that an adviser's job can be more difficult in such circumstances: should the adviser be obliged to advise that the horse or price is unsuitable, he or she will certainly need to exercise considerable tact and diplomacy.

With regard to pricing, a particular stumbling block can arise when a vendor offers to sell a horse on for what he or she paid for it – not an uncommon arrangement among friends. This may, of course, represent very good value but if, as previously mentioned, good money was paid for largely unfulfilled potential, it may represent very poor value indeed. I can, in fact, think of a case where first-time owners – advised by someone with vested interests – bought a horse from friends on this basis: although the horse proved reasonably suitable for them, the purchase price was about twice what they should have expected to pay for a suitable animal and, in my estimation, at least twice what this particular horse was worth.

This recollection serves to emphasise the fact that equine values do have a personal element; indeed, it could be argued that, ultimately, a horse is worth whatever somebody is prepared to pay for it. Of course, if this were the whole truth, it would be difficult to talk of under- or overspending but whether such a definition represents a horse's *true* value is open to question – in fact, trying to put an absolute value on a horse would be akin to juggling smoke. Moreover, if someone has been asked to advise on buying a horse, one assumption is that he or she should be better placed than the prospective purchasers to make reasonable estimations of value, and should therefore prevent them from setting their sights obviously too high or too low.

Prior to looking at any horses, therefore, it makes sense for purchaser and adviser to establish a ceiling price. This should represent what the adviser believes is a realistic price for the type of horse required, plus (if the owner can afford it) a *sensible* percentage extra. This extra will allow some room for manoeuvre should the purchaser see a horse that is a *little* expensive but really takes his or her fancy. Although flagrant overspending is just a waste of money, it is preferable for a single horse owner to pay slightly over the odds for such an animal than to buy one that 'might do' because it seems cheap.

Once all of these matters have been resolved, the search can begin for a suitable horse. It should be borne in mind that suitability, in all its aspects, becomes even more important when purchasing than when mounting a pupil for a lesson. It is usually possible, if not desirable, for riders to endure the occasional hour on an unsuitable horse – or, if not, to swap – but it is a different story when the horse is their own.

To ensure suitability, as far as one can, there are three broad areas to consider. First, as discussed previously, horse and rider should be physically compatible. Second, the horse should be sound, healthy and of reasonable conformation. Since the detail of such matters can (and does) fill a number of books, this is not the place to discuss them in depth; suffice it to say that anyone advising on purchase should be sufficiently knowledgeable to 'spin' anything with obvious drawbacks, while a good horse vet can do the rest when he or she examines the horse *before* purchase.

The third area to consider is suitability for the purchaser's declared intentions. Indeed, an adviser needs to be satisfied that these intentions are realistic in principle before trying to find a horse on which they can be put into practice. I recall a salutary comment from an eminent horse vet who

'I so enjoy a quiet hack.'! The suitability of horses to their owners' requirements

reckoned – physical considerations aside – that *the majority* of horses he examined for prospective purchasers were not well suited to their future owners' riding ability or requirements.

122

This question of suitability should be most easily resolved if the purchaser simply wants to hack out. For such a purpose it is unnecessary to obtain a horse that would win hack classes in the show ring; all that is required is one that is willing, amenable in company and safe. Where riders have competitive ambitions, however, the picture becomes rather more complex. If, for example, a pupil is just about ready to attempt local-level competition, he or she should be dissuaded from buying a novice horse 'so that we can learn together', or the sort of horse he or she might, perhaps, aspire to in several years' time. Whereas a sensible schoolmaster type could be expected to give a good grounding and aid progress, starting out with a novice or a talented but difficult type will almost certainly result in mutual deterioration. In this respect, it is very important that an adviser does not succumb to the temptation of encouraging the purchase of a horse because *he or she* would like it and be suited by it. If the chance to school, or compete on the horse has been offered, such temptation may be quite strong, but the fact remains that the horse will belong to the purchaser and must, ultimately, suit him or her. An adviser or instructor can set the scene for a great deal of friction and frustration by ignoring this fact, perhaps even to the point of falling out with the owner-pupil because the instructor feels 'his' or 'her' horse is being spoilt. It is much better to earn the respect and gratitude of pupils by helping them to find horses that *they* can enjoy to the full.

CHAPTER TWELVE

Conclusion

This book has endeavoured, essentially, to persuade instructors to recognise the needs of mature riders, and to teach them in a manner from which they will derive maximum benefit. While it is my hope that instructors will gain considerable satisfaction from introducing mature people to a new sport – or rekindling old interests – I would like to conclude by highlighting the actual benefits that teachers in particular, and the riding world in general, can gain from so doing.

The most obvious, and fundamental, advantage is the establishment of a regular and reliable customer base. If mature people enjoy their riding, find a worthwhile challenge in learning a new skill, and perhaps also see it as a therapeutic escape from a demanding lifestyle, they are likely to make considerable efforts to attend lessons on a regular basis. Furthermore, while it is not true of all, a significant proportion of mature riders have a reasonable amount of disposable income which, time permitting, may enable the keener elements to ride with some frequency and may, in due course, allow them to become horse owners and thus sources of livery income. It is also likely that mature pupils who are parents will bring interested offspring to an establishment in which they are confident: even if the cost of tuition for offspring impinges on the amount parents spend on their own riding, this arrangement lays a valuable foundation of second-generation clients.

The other main advantage is that it is often mature riders who become the backbone of the Riding Club movement. In many cases, they may be content to spend as much, if not more, time in organising as in competing. They may also be able to offer relevant organisational and business skills, and perhaps help defray running costs by offering business services at preferential rates, even providing local-level sponsorship in return for their business being advertised in show schedules. In some cases, they may have more far-reaching skills, such as professional planning knowledge or other legal qualifications, which can be instrumental in protecting or promoting the interests of riding in the locality.

Altruism and professional pride should be sufficient reasons for an instructor to give *any* pupil his or her best attention, and virtue is deemed to be its own reward. If, however, pupils, teachers and the sport of riding can all derive genuine benefit from thoughtful and committed instruction, where is the harm in that?